Greed is Dead

Paul Collier is the Professor of Economics and Public Policy at the Oxford Blavatnik School of Government. He is the author of *The Future of Capitalism*, which won the 2019 Handelsblatt Prize; *The Bottom Billion*, which won the Lionel Gelber Prize and Arthur Ross Prize of the Council on Foreign Relations; and *The Plundered Planet*, *Exodus* and *Refuge* (with Alexander Betts). Collier has served as Director of the Research Department of the World Bank, and works with governments around the world.

John Kay is one of Britain's leading economists and a fellow of St John's College, Oxford. His career has spanned academia, business, finance and public policy. He was the founding head of the Oxford Said Business School and the Institute for Fiscal Studies – Britain's most respected think tank. He is the author of *The Truth About Markets*, *Obliquity*, *Other People's Money* and other books, and for twenty years he contributed a regular column to the *Financial Times*.

PAUL COLLIER AND JOHN KAY

Greed is Dead

Politics after Individualism

PENGUIN BOOKS

PENGUIN BOOKS

UK | USA | Canada | Ireland | Australia
India | New Zealand | South Africa

Penguin Books is part of the Penguin Random House group of companies
whose addresses can be found at global.penguinrandomhouse.com

First published by Allen Lane 2020
Published with a revised Preface in Penguin Books 2021
001

Printed and bound in Great Britain by Clays Ltd, Elcograf S.p.A.

The authorized representative in the EEA is Penguin Random House Ireland,
Morrison Chambers, 32 Nassau Street, Dublin D02 YH68

A CIP catalogue record for this book is available from the British Library

ISBN: 978-0-141-99416-1

www.greenpenguin.co.uk

Penguin Random House is committed to a
sustainable future for our business, our readers
and our planet. This book is made from Forest
Stewardship Council® certified paper.

In memory of our friend Peter Sinclair, economist and gentleman, who died from COVID-19. We hope he would have appreciated this book.

'We cultivate refinement without extravagance and knowledge without effeminacy; wealth we employ more for use than for show, and place the real disgrace of poverty not in owning to the fact but in declining the struggle against it. Our public men have, besides politics, their private affairs to attend to, and our ordinary citizens, though occupied with the pursuits of industry, are still fair judges of public matters; for, unlike any other nation, regarding him who takes no part in these duties not as unambitious but as useless, we Athenians are able to judge at all events if we cannot originate, and, instead of looking on discussion as a stumbling-block in the way of action, we think it an indispensable preliminary to any wise action at all. Again, in our enterprises we present the singular spectacle of daring and deliberation, each carried to its highest point, and both united in the same persons.'*

– Pericles' funeral oration, as perhaps reported by/ perhaps written by Thucydides, *History of the Peloponnesian War* (translation, R. Crawley, 2004), Athens, 430BC

Acknowledgements

The premise of this book is that the ideas in the mind of an individual are formed through the community of people with whom they interact. We are no exception: the ideas in this book, though often new, have grown out of reading and conversing with others, both scholars in a range of disciplines and people with the knowledge that can come only from practical experience specific to purpose and context. They are too numerous to name – some of them will recognize their influence. Ideas that are original are often wrong. Being all too aware of it, we are grateful to the people who have commented on earlier drafts of this book, endeavouring to save us from ourselves. Stuart Proffitt of Allen Lane has been a superb editor, balancing encouragement with perceptive suggestions and criticism; Colin Mayer and Steve Fisher, themselves busy academics, valuably commented on the entire script, as did our wives, Pauline and Mika, who also had to put up with us as we wrestled to transform a mass of half-formed thoughts into *Greed is Dead*. Matthew Ford and Doris Nikolic not only provided invaluable research assistance but robust challenge to some of our ideas.

Contents

Preface: Why Now?   xiii

1   What is Going On Here?   1

PART I
The Triumph of Individualism

2   Individualist Economics   13
3   Rights   29
4   From Civil Rights to Expressive Identity   37

PART II
Government: Symptoms of Distress

5   The Rise and Fall of the Paternal State   51
6   Shifting Political Tectonic Plates   64
7   How Labour Lost the Working Class   75

PART III
Community

8   Our Communitarian Nature   91
9   Communitarian Governance   101
10   Communitarian Politics   112
11   Communitarianism, Markets and Business   125
12   Communities of Place   138
     Epilogue: Shelter from the Storm   151

Notes   157
Further Reading   165
Bibliography   169
Index   181

Preface: Why Now?

We completed the first edition of *Greed is Dead* in the spring of 2020, as the first wave of COVID-19 spread around the world. We planned the book, of course, before anyone had heard of the virus. But there are themes in our previous work which seem apposite, both to the immediate crisis and to the longer-term political outlook. Paul's recent book *The Future of Capitalism* – a response to Britain's widening divergences – is about restoring social cohesion. John's recent book with Mervyn King, *Radical Uncertainty*, rejects the idea that all uncertainty can be described probabilistically. The exaggerated faith in models which arose contributed directly to the global financial crisis. These two themes, radical uncertainty and social cohesion, intertwine, and are central to our book. An exaggerated belief in the power of models to explain our world has imbued political and business leaders with overconfidence. The rise of individualism has weakened the capacity of society to work together for common purposes. And the two have interacted: leaders thought they knew what to do, but distrusted people as being too selfish to cooperate, so they relied on incentives linked to scrutiny. Both these themes, which made our collaboration a natural one, turned out to be relevant to understanding the impact of COVID-19 and the political responses to it.

WHAT DID WE ALL LEARN FROM COVID?

Dealing with the pandemic required a paradoxical combination of social distancing and social solidarity. We needed to keep apart to avoid spreading the virus; we needed to come together to deal with its consequences. We were deprived of opportunities to support our friends and relatives, or to help our colleagues at work; but we volunteered to ferry supplies and clapped for carers. In this book, we stress the value of and need for solidarity even in less troubled times. As vaccination seems to release societies from the anxieties of COVID, we find reasons for optimism that such solidarity can be restored. In the lessons from the pandemic, we have seen forceful reminders of the importance of community.

We do not know the epidemiology of COVID, and nor does anyone else. There are several epidemiologists who make large claims to knowledge – their models are capable of making clear predictions. But their models disagree. Such models can do no more than identify the key parameters – the number of people each infected person infects, and the proportion of those infected who suffer serious illness. But at the start of the pandemic, we did not even roughly know the size of these parameters. We could only infer their changing values after the event. We thus see both the uses and limitations of models when public policy faces radical uncertainty.

In October 2019, Johns Hopkins University published a three-year study of the relative capacity of different countries to deal with pandemics. The three countries best prepared were supposedly the United States, Britain and the Netherlands. As the virus spread, these three were among the countries most seriously affected. Social and political factors influencing responses turned out to be far more significant than the technical and objective factors Johns Hopkins had chosen to quantify. The mortality rate from COVID is specific to age, so, for many people, adhering to social distancing and accepting vaccination helps others more than it helps themselves. Across the world, the consequences of variations in the relative power of the state, the influence of culture and values, and the sense of community relative to the strength of individualist sentiments, go to the very heart of the issues discussed in this book.

The very different effects of policies and behaviour in different countries are already sufficient to begin to pose questions and propose hypotheses. The best measure of the medical impact is probably the level of excess deaths – how many more people died than would have been expected to die in a 'normal' year. This indicator recognizes that the elderly and frail who make up the majority of COVID fatalities may die with COVID but not of it, and also recognizes the tragedy of people whose cancers went undiagnosed or strokes untreated because hospitals were overloaded or because fear of COVID or a misguided sense of solidarity deterred them from seeking timely medical assistance. The count of excess deaths takes no account, of course, of the other social and economic costs of the disease, and the measures taken to restrict its spread: the venues closed, the businesses folding or operating below capacity, the school days lost.

Some countries reported no or negligible numbers of excess deaths. Although the virus originated in China, most of these countries are in Asia and Australasia. All these states imposed tight restrictions on internal and external movement and implemented systems to trace the contacts of infected people. Taiwan, South Korea and Singapore deployed to good effect the technological efficiency of a powerful state and the values of societies that prize family and community ahead of the individual. The Nordic countries also experienced few deaths, benefiting from lockdowns reinforced by high levels of social cohesion; Sweden, which imposed few restrictions, did much worse in terms of mortality than its Scandinavian neighbours, but better in economic consequences than most other European countries. Denmark looks to have got the balance right: government actions that were sufficiently decisive to alert citizens to the importance of behaving responsibly to achieve a new common purpose. Australia and New Zealand benefited from the ease with which they could control their borders, and New Zealand escaped the virus almost entirely.

Thus very different styles of leadership were illustrated. Totalitarian China, where the outbreak began, appears to have brought the disease under control relatively quickly. Sweden's political leaders remained in the background, relying on scientists to make and explain policy, while New Zealand's Jacinta Ardern's finely tuned ear for the public mood and emphasis upon mutual responsibility – 'we are a team of 5 million' – enabled her government to carry public opinion in taking radical measures. Viktor Orbán took the opportunity to gather unlimited power to himself, but the virus defied him even if the Hungarian press could not.

The countries worst affected by the virus were India and in Latin America. Europe and North America were also badly hit, but there was a wide range of responses and experiences. In mid 2020, the research group More in Common undertook an international survey of public reaction to the events.[1] Most people said that they had observed the restrictions – and that other people had done so. They said that one feature of communitarian behaviour – concern for others – had increased, but another – their trust in others – had declined. Their countries were more divided, they thought. France certainly was: most French people believed that while they themselves had generally observed the restrictions, most other people had not.

The United States was an outlier in almost every respect. It was the only country surveyed in which people did not think concern for others had risen, and – along with France – one in which trust in the healthcare system had declined rather than increased. Every issue of everyday life seemed tainted by partisanship. Even on a trivially mundane question – 'would you be comfortable having a haircut during the pandemic?' – views were politically polarized: 72 per cent of Republicans replied 'yes', but only 37 per cent of Democrats did so.[2] Facing the same medical information, Republican governors opened their states and their schools; Democrat governors closed theirs down.

THE NEW CULTURE WARS

The policy disagreements in America were driven not by information but by deep new cultural conflicts that reached their zenith in January 2021. Had the political leaders swapped their policies on restrictions, Republicans and Democrats might simply have swapped their views on haircuts. Extraordinary photographs appeared in newspapers around the world and on social media. A man walked through the Capitol building wearing a Star Wars costume and Viking horns; another carried a Confederate flag; another was sitting in the office of Nancy Pelosi, Speaker of the US House of Representatives, his feet on her desk. The rioters videoed themselves and beamed footage around the world. The event was the epitome of the expressive individualism we critique in this book, the celebration of the self in purported support of a political cause.

But expressive individualism was characteristic of the progressive left as well as the alt-right:

> As J and his team heaved the mast vertical, a huge cheer rang out across Oxford Circus. J commented 'hearing that cheer was one of the best feelings I ever had' … With DJs on the deck, barnacles locked-on to the keel, and a sea of rebels dancing and leafleting and making speeches around its hull, the boat represented the entire XR [Extinction Rebellion] ecosystem in one heaving, joyous, living entity.[3]

'J' was a leader of a group of climate-change activists, and the mast belonged to a pink boat which they had placed at Oxford Circus in April 2019 in central London, seriously disrupting the city's traffic for several days.

If the event's organizers had hoped to stoke a culture war, they succeeded. Home Secretary Priti Patel responded, 'The very criminals who disrupt our free society must be stopped. Together we must all stand firm against the guerrilla tactics of Extinction Rebellion.'[4] Of course, Patel's overreaction stimulated further response, as 'kill the bill' protests blocked streets with protestors opposing her legislation to extend police powers to prevent mass gatherings.

The self-righteous narcissism of 'activists' sometimes entails minor self-abnegation – 'veganuary' in 2021 was followed by Toni Petersson using an interval in the Super Bowl to sing 'wow, wow, no cow' from the middle of a field of oats – but purely symbolic virtue-signalling has become a preoccupation in universities. John began the study of economics in the David Hume Tower. The University of Edinburgh's ugliest building was named for its most distinguished alumnus, the eighteenth-century philosopher and friend of Adam Smith, who did so much to lay the foundations of modern social and political thought. But it is the David Hume Tower no longer; all reference to Hume has been deleted. Not because he has risen from the grave to protest against the destruction of the magnificent George Square, a product in stone of that Scottish enlightenment, in favour of the brutalist building which carried his name. No; the problem is Hume's view on race. In a footnote to a publication of 1753, he had observed that 'I am apt to suspect the negroes to be naturally inferior to the whites.' As the university's leading historian pointed out, this view, which we now know to be wrong, was commonly held in the eighteenth century.[5] Even Smith himself is threatened with cancellation; his magnum opus had described slavery as 'ubiquitous and inevitable', though 'apt to be less profitable than free labour'. Perhaps a less than ringing endorsement of the practice; but sufficient to require a committee of Edinburgh City Council to review whether public commemoration of the author of the *Wealth of Nations* remains appropriate.

The common feature of all these activities is that they are performative – the purpose of the protest is the protest, and the sense of virtue, or perhaps simply the fun, they offer to the individuals engaged in them. Two weeks after the Capitol Hill break in, Joe Biden was nevertheless inaugurated as President. The police towed the pink boat away from Oxford Circus, leaving the planet no cooler than before. And the racism of the Minneapolis Police Department is not relieved by the University of Edinburgh's rescission of its homage to David Hume. Only Ms Patel's illiberal legislation survives.

The Capitol Hill rioters and the Oxford Circus revellers are communities of a sort. But they are not the communities of mutual assistance, developing collective intelligence through the exchange of ideas and knowledge, which we applaud in this book. They are communities of people who talk mainly to each other, reassuring themselves of their own rightness, and asserting the moral superiority of their own shared identities. The resulting polarization is destructive of the wider communities from which a cohesive society is built. The campaigners who secured the abolition of the slave trade built a coalition to advance their cause; the mob who pull down statues do not care that they alienate a large public that views British history with more pride than shame.

The new culture wars are being fought out not just between the political parties, but within them. They have become especially severe within the parties of the left. Britain's Labour Party is now an untenable coalition of 'progressives' engaged in virtue signalling and the party's traditional working-class base, an electorate more repelled than attracted by these signals. Having gone unremarked for years, the divorce from the working class is now documented in a flood of new studies. Trade unionist Paul Embery is the author of *Despised*:

Why the Modern Left Loathes the Working Class (2020). Deborah Mattinson's *Beyond the Red Wall* (2020) convinces by eschewing theorizing in favour of asking hundreds of Red Wall voters why they had switched their vote: views such as, 'I think we can be the best again, and that will bring employment back' (p. 176). Such pride in the past and ambition for an enterprising future diverges radically from the perspective of Labour's metropolitan activists, for whom David Hume and Adam Smith are figures to be ashamed of rather than admired. Yet, as Jon Cruddas, a rare working-class Labour MP, argues in *The Dignity of Labour* (2021), it is those activists, not the working class, which now dominate the party.

We have seen this in the reaction to our book. Since the first edition we have engaged with many individuals and groups across business and finance, NGOs and politics. Yet amid the reactions to our politically centrist message, written primarily for the left, there has been one deafening silence: no publication on the left has reviewed it. The left has become such a vicious forum that the centrist majority who voted for Keir Starmer as leader has not dared publicly to engage with a book that many in that majority privately tell us they appreciate.

And the cautious attempt of Keir Starmer to reposition the party has paid the price of antagonizing the activists without convincing the voters. The exit of Jeremy Corbyn briefly revived its fortunes. But as we write, Labour support in the opinion polls has relapsed to the level of its disastrous election of 2019. This slump has happened despite the confusion of Brexit and the frequently inept government response to the pandemic. Opinion polls can be shrugged off, but not political earthquakes. The once-safe Labour seat of Hartlepool has fallen in a mid-term by-election to the Conservatives. For the Opposition to lose a seat to the governing party in mid term is a once-in-a-generation event. Labour's leaders can no longer prevaricate over the stark choice between its activist membership and the voters who have abandoned it.

President Biden faces the same problem, relieved only for a time by the integrity and competence which so clearly distinguishes him from his predecessor. The 'progressive' left of his party is even more strident than their European equivalents; the alienation of the traditional blue-collar base of the Democratic party yet more extreme than in the UK.

The first-past-the-post electoral systems of Britain and the US have so far enabled the two established parties in each country to maintain dominance of the electoral process. In continental Europe, these structures are breaking down as new and fringe parties win support – Greens, Macron's centrist En Marche, extremes of left and right. In France, the socialist party which won election as recently as 2012 struggles to win discernable poll ratings, while the main beneficiary has been the far right. According to a new poll, among youth aged 18–25, Le Pen leads Macron by 2-to-1 with nobody else in sight.

Yet we see solid grounds for optimism. Despite the mindless posturing of activists there is a ferment of genuinely new ideas and thoughtful argument. As we write, squalid manifestations of greed still surround us. But after forty years of rising selfishness, the 2020s may represent Peak Greed. From the extremities of self-absorption we are returning to community. This is not idle dreaming; as we show in this book, the tide is on the turn.

The rise of selfishness found justification in a ramshackle intellectual edifice. On the political right the glorification of individualism originated in a mistaken turn in economics: a misreading of evolutionary biology that trivialized human motivation and exaggerated human knowledge. The political left, which had for long valued solidarity, came instead to frame its arguments in terms of individual rights – a mistaken turn in moral philosophy that set up contests of grievance and claimed to ground them in newly discovered eternal moral truths. Though politically uncomfortable bedfellows, both ideas relegated the role of community and dismissed radical uncertainty. The only actors were individuals with rights and the state with obligations; the smartest knew best and should take the decisions.

That shaky edifice is now rapidly disintegrating. *Greed is Dead* is but a small part of a revolution across science, social science and the humanities that is rapidly restoring community to its central role in enabling societies to thrive. In our own subject of economics, the business schools which for decades taught ambitious young executives that 'greed is good' are now questioning it. *Reimagining Capitalism* (2020) comes from the pen of Rebecca Henderson, Harvard Business School's prestigious University Professor. *The Third Pillar* (2019), comes from Milton Friedman's home base, Chicago; written not by some young renegade but by its business school's distinguished professor, Raghu Rajan. The pillars on which successful societies depend are not just individuals and the state: the third vital pillar is community, which Rajan argues has been missing. From our own home base of Oxford, comes *Prosperity: Better Business Makes the Greater Good*, by Colin Mayer, who succeeded John as the Director of our business school. In parallel, exaggerated confidence in the rule of the smart was punctured first by events – the Global Financial Crisis – shortly followed by the rediscovery of radical uncertainty (Minsky, 2013; Kay and King, 2020).

In science, Joe Henrich's *The Secret of Our Success* (2016) and *The Weirdest People* (2020) set out the evolutionary evidence that individual behaviour is largely set not by personal greed but by the collective mind of a community. Far from having evolved to be individually 'smart', the secret of our success is to imagine, innovate and learn communally from experiments. Henrich is the director of Harvard's Department of Evolutionary Biology, whose critique of a crude 'survival of the fittest' is reinforced in *Blueprint* (2019), by Yale's Nicholas Christakis, and by Oxford physiologist Denis Noble's 'The Illusions of the Modern Synthesis' in *Biosemiotics*, March 2021.

In philosophy, both the blind consequentialism of utilitarianism and the mental gymnastics of Rawls' 'distributive justice' have been supplanted. In *The Tyranny of Merit* (2020), Michael Sandel sets out the concept of 'contributive justice' – a dense web of mutual obligations within a community from which rights emerge. Sandel is the world's most influential moral philosopher, his online lectures from Harvard followed by millions. Jonathan Sacks, the former Chief Rabbi of the UK, presented arguments similar to ours, but from a very different perspective, in *Morality: Restoring the Common Good in Divided Times* (2020). We were sad to learn of his death soon after the publication of his illuminating book.

In political science, Robert Putnam's *The Upswing* (2020) provides a brilliant analysis of the shifting American balance between individualism and community over the past 150 years. The 'upswing' of his title is the revival of community that began in towns across America around 1900, a revival reinforced nationally by the pragmatic leadership of Theodore Roosevelt. Communitarianism peaked in the early

1960s, from which began an accelerating descent into selfish and ideological individualism. Putnam is the world's most renowned political sociologist. This evidence is deepened in *Virtue Politics* (2020), by his Harvard colleague the historian James Hankins, who draws an analogy between Theodore Roosevelt's Progressive Movement and the social origins of the Italian Renaissance. Both Putnam and Hankins describe inflection points – the rare moments when the direction of social change is reversed. Putnam attributes them to the conjunction of an intellectual revolution with a mortal global shock that vindicates the new ideas.

COVID may have helped us reach one of these rare moments. The 'smart' leaders who claimed to know what to do about COVID have been humiliated: it has been a classic instance of radical uncertainty. And of communitarianism: COVID has turned out to depend upon the willing compliance of the members of each local community to safeguard their neighbours. Denmark virtually avoided COVID through willing compliance; North Korea is plunging into famine despite the extremities of state coercion.

Domestically, the changing arena of British politics is inescapable. There is wide recognition of the need to reverse the extreme concentration of good jobs in London, and the divorce of the Labour Party from the working class. Since much of the divergence of the regions from London happened under Labour governments, the two issues are clearly intertwined. The voices of a metropolitan elite had more influence on Labour's priorities than its traditional base.

Since 1980, economic opportunities in Britain's regions have diverged dramatically from those in London – we have become a complete outlier in the OECD in our degree of regional inequality. Unsurprisingly, reversing this has become the top post-COVID priority: indeed, according to recent opinion polls not only does it have overwhelming public approval, but it is the only priority accepted by a majority of the population with wide support across the political spectrum. We know that the recent skew to London was avoidable, and we also know that it has not achieved faster national growth – we only have to look at other countries to see that. But, unfortunately, reversing this divergence is an example of radical uncertainty – we don't know in detail how to do it. We do, however, know how not to do it: it cannot be done to the regions by Whitehall. Only communitarian governance – a common purpose agreed and guided by a community – has the context-specific knowledge needed for learning by experiment. That the problem of regional divergence reflects these principles of radical uncertainty and communitarianism is not due to chance. We face this regional problem because Britain has the most over-centralized governance, both political and commercial, in the OECD. We have been run by overconfident 'smart' leaders in London who decided both public policy and the allocation of finance. Public expenditure on everything from infrastructure and research to the arts has massively favoured London. Private finance for business, both start-ups and scale-ups, was also wildly skewed: two-thirds of venture capital for small firms goes to London and the south-east, which accounts for only one fifth of the nation's population. Popular anger at this situation is fully justified.

Having lived through momentous crises, we are at last looking to the future, in a much-changed world. The combination of individual selfishness and overconfident top-down management has badly damaged our societies. But the future can be different. There is a new eagerness for agency, and a new recognition that the accumulated anxieties from past neglect can only be addressed by coming together. You can be part of that process of change: we have written this book to help you do so. This paperback edition of *Greed is Dead* appears at a critical moment.

I

What is Going On Here?

'I celebrate myself, and sing myself'
Walt Whitman, 'Song of Myself'

We live in societies saturated in selfishness. So how can we say that 'greed is dead'? What we mean is that the extreme individualism embraced by many prominent and successful people in recent decades, and which sought justification in terms of merit or celebrity, is no longer intellectually tenable. Humans are naturally prosocial, and exhibitionist greed is both grating and contagious. The excessive financial demands of businesspeople and the claims of identity politics, the preening and posturing of Trump and Putin, Bolsonaro and Kim Jong Un, and the rise of the reality-TV star and the 'influencer' share a central characteristic – it's all about *me*. Some are greedy for money, others greedy for attention. The libertarian fantasies of Silicon Valley rely on similar selfish motivation. And it has all gone much too far.

Successive presidential speeches mark the passage from post-war communitarianism to the subsequent rise of individualism. In 1960, John F. Kennedy, who had defeated Richard Nixon to become President, delivered an inaugural address that became the iconic statement of communitarian politics. 'And so, my fellow Americans: ask not what your country can do for you – ask what you can do for your country.'[1] By 1973, Kennedy was dead and Nixon was delivering his second inaugural speech. Nixon's appeal to his countrymen began by echoing Kennedy's sentiment: 'let each of us ask – not just what will government do for me . . .' Yet what followed was decidedly less inspirational: '. . . but what can I do for myself?'[2]

Forty years later, that age of individualism had reached ugly maturity. Campaigning for re-election in 2012, President Obama was captured in what the *Wall Street Journal* described as 'a burst of ideological candor . . . Rarely do politicians so clearly reveal their core beliefs.'[3] For the rabid talk-show host Rush Limbaugh, this was 'the most telling moment of Obama's presidency'.[4] What had Obama revealed in his off-the-cuff remarks?

> If you were successful, somebody along the line gave you some help. There was a great teacher somewhere in your life. Somebody helped to create this unbelievable American system that we have that allowed you to thrive. Somebody invested in roads and bridges. If you've got a business – you didn't build that. Somebody else made that happen. The Internet didn't get invented on its own. Government research created the Internet so that all the companies make money off the Internet. The point is, that when we succeed, we succeed because of our individual initiative, but also because we do things together.[5]

Shocked by this banal statement of the obvious? Republicans were: their convention devoted an entire day to celebrating small-business owners, swaying with pride as country-music performer Lane Turner sang, 'I Built It'. In the business world, extreme individualism manifests as a confident presumption of *material* entitlement – 'I built it: I deserve it.' Obama had transgressed by his modest qualification to *possessive* individualism – the notion originating with John Locke that property rights are acquired, not from some process of social cooperation and consent, but by mixing one's labour with some resource. The frontier spirit which encloses ground and defends it with a gun against neighbours, the forces of the state and the indigenous population.

And Obama's successor would represent the apotheosis of individualism. Since 2017, the office once held by great statesmen such as Lincoln and Roosevelt has been occupied by someone whose claims to statesmanship exist only in his own mind. No longer as head of state would he symbolize the dignity of a great nation – as Eisenhower or Reagan had done, or as the Queen continues to do. For President Trump, it was all about *me*.

Trump had achieved fame through reality TV. But he had at least built things (not always paying for them). *Expressive* individualism stands free even of that: Paris Hilton and the Kardashians, PewDiePie and James Charles are famous only for being themselves. And those among them who decry the selfish materialism of modern business are not averse to relishing their assertion of moral superiority. Today it appears that no celebrity can accept an award without delivering a condescending homily to a fawning audience.

In universities, similar claims of moral superiority derive from the presumption of *intellectual* entitlement intrinsic to meritocracy: 'I'm clever so *I* know best.' A presumption so strong that its beneficiaries not only do not wish to hear dissent but seek to suppress it. The unenlightened are not to be dignified with reasoned argument but are the proper subject of personal abuse – they are fascists, homophobes, racists, transphobes, climate-change deniers. In the media and among public-sector professionals, an equivalent claim to moral superiority found a different origin. Exemplified by the passionate outrage expressed in a newspaper column or protest meeting, the *intensity of feeling* was for many the measure of moral worth. We are right because we are better people and we take every opportunity to tell you so.

This ugly stridency is the product of an extreme elite individualism – the rise of the self at the expense of community – which has taken over much of modern political and cultural thought. Yet the more we learn about our evolution, our psychology, our anthropology, about our history as a species – and modern research has greatly illuminated all these subjects – the clearer it becomes that this individualism fails to recognize the fundamentals of humanity.

Our human nature has given us a unique capacity for mutuality. We are (mostly) not saints, but nor (mostly) are we sociopaths. In the complex modern world we could not thrive without an exceptional capacity for mutuality: more fundamentally, without that capacity we could never have created the complexity that has enabled modernity. A healthy society is a vast web of cooperative activity sustained by mutual kindnesses and obligations. Some of the interdependencies are between individuals, but most involve people in groups – firms, local governments, colleges, communities and families. Most of these interrelationships are based on unwritten understandings, not legal documents.

Cumulatively, the quality of these interrelationships makes the difference between societies that thrive and those paralysed by discord; the difference between prosperous economies and primitive ones where time is mostly spent scratching a living through the individual search for food and fuel. But the capacity to build and sustain such webs of interrelationship must be nurtured: the glorification of the self by the successful has done the opposite.

Humans both cooperate and compete – and each of these capacities is capable of being both constructive and destructive. We can cooperate constructively to create complex webs of social and economic relationships which enhance our consumption, our work and our leisure, while sheltering us in times of adversity; or destructively, to impose our religions and political and economic values on other groups and other nations and steal their resources. We can compete constructively to innovate in the economy, the arts, and in building better and more fulfilling lives; or destructively, to gain priority access to scarce resources. And in the last two centuries humans have done all these things on an unprecedented scale.

Successful societies – durable, prosperous and meeting the needs of their citizens – are those which have created institutions which channel both cooperation and competition into positive channels, to achieve complex goals of general benefit. They are pluralist, but their pluralism is disciplined. As Obama explained, 'when we succeed, we succeed because of our individual initiative, but also because we do things together'.

In this book, we describe two clusters of individualist thought, one promoted by economists, the other by lawyers. The economic cluster begins with the assertion of entitlement based on property rights derived from one's own efforts – *possessive individualism*. This belief is then ethically vindicated by *market fundamentalism* – the belief that economies prosper by imposing as few restrictions as possible on the ability of financiers and businesspeople to dispose of their property. These doctrines have been a gift for the financially successful.

'Greed is all right, by the way. I want you to know that. I think greed is healthy. You can be greedy and still feel good about yourself.'[6] Ivan Boesky, later convicted of insider trading, explained this to commencing MBA students at Berkeley in 1986, his words paraphrased the following year by Michael Douglas in the film *Wall Street* as 'Greed is good!' But what is 'good'? The final belief in this cluster is the criterion by which social outcomes should be judged: *utilitarian individualism*. This is the idea that the general good is simply the sum of the good of individuals.

Another cluster of individualist ideas is built around claims of entitlement: 'my rights!' – a gift for those who want privilege but not obligations to others. The American and French revolutions emphasized rights – the self-evident truths of the Declaration of Independence, the proclamation of the demands of *liberté, égalité, fraternité*. The rise of the modern culture of rights began with the 1948 United Nations Declaration of Human Rights. More recently, assertions of rights have taken a more strident turn. The self-righteous activist shares with the current President of the United States a love of *expressive individualism* – the emphasis on the assertion of the self at the expense of identification with families, neighbours, colleagues and fellow citizens. The only communities these activists recognize are communities of people like themselves. Within these communities, self-expression is performative – protest and outrage – its quality judged by the intensity of passion rather than the depth of knowledge. Almost incredibly, both 'woke' students at elite universities and the current President of the United States see themselves as victims – the former oppressed by white male privilege, the latter harassed by witch hunts, 'fake news' and attempted coups.

These multiple strands of individualist thought are related, but distinct, and it is possible, and common, to believe in some but not others. Jeremy Bentham, one of the first and most articulate proponents of utilitarian individualism, dismissed natural rights as 'nonsense on stilts'; conversely, the culture of rights tends to reject the consequentialism – what will be the practical effects of this decision? – which is central to utilitarianism.[7] The pursuit of individualism leads in many different and sometimes incompatible directions. The market fundamentalist who is loud in defence of private property rights, and who sings along to 'I Built It' at Republican rallies, has not much in common with the enthusiast for identity politics who marches under the banner 'Proud to be gay'. But both individuals demonstrate a common emphasis on the self; for both, it is all about *me*. And sometimes, in a perversion of community – the purpose of cooperation being destructive of others – a particular type of individualist will band together to make demands on everybody else. The financially successful will lobby for tax cuts; the great-grandchildren of victim groups will demand reparations.

Unlike Bentham, the authors do not dismiss any of these strands of thought as intrinsically nonsensical. But when taken to extremes these diverse strands of individualism underpin this new emphasis on the self. Their flaws become destructive, their worldview shrivels society to individuals who have rights and the state which has obligations. This worldview both underestimates the central role of willing cooperative activity in contributing to social and economic life, and imposes on the state burdens which it has been unable to bear.

We do not believe that free markets produce the best of all possible worlds, but we are sure that the state direction of economic activity does not do so either. We think it important that basic freedoms are enshrined in law, but we also recognize that property rights are social constructs rather than entitlements derived from a state of nature, and need to be justified as well as upheld. We think that to describe the fulfilment of social and economic aspirations as human rights undermines the empathy and solidarity on which support for the poor and underprivileged depends.

People should be applauded and protected for their roles both as individuals and in communities. Humans are social animals, wanting to belong, and to gain the good opinion of others. Modern evolutionary biology, far from lending support to the premises of individualism, undermines them. Human lives are dominated by organisms which are neither individual nor statist: family, friends, clubs and associations – and the businesses people buy from, and the organizations in which people work.

Human capacity to communicate far exceeds that of any other species. We use our language skills to argue and debate, to exhort and to forge mutual obligations. We are imaginative. That imagination enables us to put ourselves in the position of others – it is the basis of our capacity for empathy. Our imagination is also the fount both of our ambitious purposes and of the creativity of our attempts to achieve them. Since our ambitions exceed our knowledge, we experience uncertainty. Humans cope with that uncertainty by learning from each other: communities build collective knowledge that guides their members. This accumulated knowledge becomes the source of much wisdom and some error.

The founding father of economics, Adam Smith, recognized that humans are characterized by this complex mixture of selfishness and empathy, aspiration and ingenuity, learning and bewilderment, competition and cooperation; and that our economic behaviour is shaped by all these factors. But as later generations of economists developed his ideas on markets, they lost sight of his understanding of human beings. Indeed, a popular modern image of Smith treats him as the prophet of self-interested individualism, the intellectual proponent of the philosophy that 'greed is good'. Markets are seen not as mechanisms for mutually beneficial exchange but places where people try to outsmart each other for their individual profit. Politics is seen not as a means of mediating good outcomes for all, but as an arena for shouting matches between the occupants of echo chambers each inhabited only by holders of common views.

The modern penchant for individualism treats markets and politics as disjoint mechanisms for reconciling individual interests. And so, understandably, both markets and politics are now held in contempt. Communities have been scarred, and those scars are manifest in our politics and our states. The new politics manifests itself across the developed world. It thrives on grievances, some well founded, others imagined or manufactured; its resentments and triumphalism have been tearing societies apart. The new elite of activists who took control of the parties of both left and right were seduced by these ideologies of individualism, supplanting the postwar policy agenda that had been shaped pragmatically to address working-class priorities.

Working-class voters have lost faith in the traditional parties of the left. In 1945 the British working class elected Labour's Attlee, and in 1948 the American working class elected the Democrat Truman. In 2019 Labour would lose Don Valley, a working-class constituency which had reliably returned a Labour MP for a hundred years, and Stoke-on-Trent North, which had never elected a member from any other party, and these were among many similar upsets. The 'rustbelt' states of Ohio, Michigan and Pennsylvania, which contained many areas of deprivation, put Trump in the White House.

But the old parties of the right had, and have, problems too. In the 1980s they had found a new ideology in market fundamentalism, but one with no resonance with most voters. Nor with traditional conservatives, who were resistant to social change, and attached to institutions such as churches and the military. As this ideology proved unsuccessful as well as unpopular, unconventional new leaders with the charisma to communicate effectively have seized the moment to reset the agenda. Some, like Boris Johnson and Emmanuel Macron, are intelligent men with aspirations to help their societies. But there is also Donald Trump, whose initial strategy of using a campaign for self-promotion ended in the pyrrhic victory of power without purpose; and illiberal figures such as Viktor Orbán, Jarosław Kaczyński, Norbert Hofer and Matteo Salvini, whose purpose is all too clear.

A few modern philosophers have resisted the individualistic emphasis in recent thought. They reject the notion that individuals have identities, preferences, rights and obligations that are separable from the particular society in which they live. In an Aristotelian tradition, they believe that individuals achieve fulfilment through their relationships with others and their contribution to civic virtues. The moral load of individuals and the associations they form is not a burden but an essential part of their fulfilment.

But these communitarian philosophers are wary of economics, sharing a belief that community is being eroded by the values and practices of the market. We are communitarians and economists, and the central argument of this book is to reconcile our communities and our economies. We believe that successful businesses are themselves communities. We see no inherent tension between community and market: markets can function effectively only when embedded in a network of social relations. Many businesses pay lip-service to this view of commerce as a social institution: 'every person at Goldman Sachs is a steward to our heritage of client service and our reputation as an ethical company'.[8] But there is a disjunction between occasional rhetoric and frequent reality which – as with that claim – teeters on the brink of self-parody.

Or beyond. In 2019 WeWork, a serviced-office provider founded by fantasist Adam Neumann, filed to offer its shares to the public. Neumann claimed that he would transform the world of work, and convinced his Japanese and Saudi backers to value the nascent company at an astounding $47 billion. Neumann *was* WeWork: the prospectus referred to 'community' 150 times, but to Neumann himself 169 times.[9] But WeWork wasn't Neumann. He had purported to sell the trademark 'We' to the business he controlled: the word 'We' was now apparently owned by 'Me!'[10] This turned out to be greed too much for the markets – the offer of shares to new investors was greeted with appropriate derision. But it was not greed too much for Neumann: his chastened backers paid him over $1 billion to go away.[11]* Neumann's combination of virtue signalling about 'community' with unrestrained self-promotion and personal enrichment encapsulated a view of the world – a view whose time has passed.

* At the time of writing it appears that Softbank may be walking away from this deal.

PART I
The Triumph of Individualism

2

Individualist Economics

'The immediate "common sense" answer to the question "what will an economy motivated by individual greed and controlled by a very large number of different agents look like?" is probably: There will be chaos . . . quite a different answer has long been claimed true . . . In attempting to answer the question "Could it be true?" we learn a good deal about how it might not be true.'

         – K. J. Arrow and F. H. Hahn, *General Competitive Analysis*, 1983

Economics hasn't always celebrated business greed. Inspired by the tragedy of the Depression, *The General Theory of Employment, Interest and Money*, published by John Maynard Keynes in 1936, had a profound influence on governments after the Second World War. Policy-makers were anxious that the unemployment that had followed the First World War should not be repeated. The Keynesian message that full employment depended upon active management of demand by the state fitted with the more general confidence in state management which followed the war.

Keynesian ideas also became, for a time, dominant in the academic world. Robin Matthews, senior professor at Oxford when we were there as young economists, wrote an article in 1968 asking, 'Why has Britain had full employment since the war?' His answer congratulated his Treasury colleagues on their demand-management skills. The 'regulator' – not a supervisor but a fiscal device – empowered government to raise or lower taxes by modest amounts at any time in order to 'fine-tune' demand and avoid high levels of either inflation or unemployment. But Matthews' article was already out of date by the time it was published.[1]

By the 1970s rising inflation, and cycles of 'stop–go', revealed the limitations of demand management. Some academic economists who had never accepted Keynesian ideas had already begun to rebuild classical economic thinking on more rigorous foundations, and the policy failures which became acute after the 1973 oil shock gave their arguments a ready audience among politicians and business-people. For the first time, the principal intellectual challenges to the orthodoxies of the political consensus came not from the left but from the right. Strong new claims were made for an economic system based on free exchange under well-defined property rights. There was an economic rationale – the outcomes of such a process were efficient. And a moral rationale – the outcomes of such a process were just.

Taken together, these arguments provided both a pragmatic and a philosophical basis for an ideology which acquiesced in, or even embraced, greed as a dominant human motivation, which believed that most policy issues had market-based solutions, and which favoured only the most minimal regulation. And from 1989 this ideology gained strength from the collapse of the dominant intellectual alternative offered by the left. The Berlin Wall fell, the Soviet Union disintegrated and the scale of communism's social and economic failure became evident. As the twentieth century drew to a close the scene was set for this market fundamentalism to dominate economic policy.

The practical workhorse of market fundamentalism was Economic Man, an unappealing mammal who responded only to financial incentives. Greedy, selfish and potentially lazy, he exemplified *possessive individualism*. And smart: he knew all that was knowable. In the key phrase used by some economists, he 'knew the model' that described how the world worked. And the model showed that individual greed could be harnessed through the miracle of the market to maximize the potential of the economy. (We describe its tenets more fully in the Annex to this chapter.) As Arrow and Hahn had described, the models properly understood are useful as much for what they teach about the limits of markets as for what we learn about their strengths.

For the right, these ideas provided an intellectual basis for the revolution in everyday thinking about politics and economics brought about by the rise of Thatcher and Reagan. Of course, most of the advocates of market fundamentalism had not reached this conclusion by careful perusal of the complex mathematics of theoretical economists and the wordy treatises of legal scholars. They had simply recognized the potential benefits to themselves of the application of the market fundamentalist doctrine. Yet the academic economic community – or parts of it – drew closer to the business and financial community than ever before. Perhaps for the first time, a group of rich men understood that the promotion of academic research, some of it quite esoteric in nature, could be deployed to their advantage. They financed new think tanks, entities which had historically mostly been identified with the political left.* The Institute of Economic Affairs was a pioneer in the UK in promoting free-market ideas, followed in the US by institutions such as the American Enterprise Institute and the Heritage Foundation.

Increasingly well funded, these economists pressed on, making fresh insights. Not only were humans supposedly selfish in their *economic* behaviour; selfishness was presumed to pervade all aspects of their lives. For Gary Becker, 'human behavior can be regarded as involving participants who maximize their utility from a stable set of preferences and accumulate an optimal amount of information and other inputs in a variety of markets. If this argument is correct, the economic approach provides a unified framework for understanding behavior that has long been sought by and eluded Bentham, Comte, Marx, and others.'[2] This was indeed an ambitious claim. Extending the analysis to all aspects of human life generated some astounding insights, such as this analysis of the exchange of gifts at Christmas: since the gifts typically cost the buyer more than what their recipients would have been willing to pay for them, gift-giving at Christmas is a utility-reducing

---

* The Fabian Society, so named after the Roman general Fabius, who had favoured slow, persistent harassment over frontal attack, was founded in England in 1884 by early socialist luminaries such as Sydney and Beatrice Webb, Bernard Shaw and H. G. Wells. The term 'think tank' seems to have been invented to describe independent research organizations such as the Rand Corporation but now mostly has a political interpretation.

anachronism.[3] In 1992 Becker would receive the Nobel Prize 'for having extended the domain of microeconomic analysis to a wide range of human behaviour and interaction'.[4] As indeed he had: Bentham, Comte and Marx would surely have been impressed. Though they might have wondered how much such extension actually *illuminated* that human behaviour and interaction.

There were still a few things that money could not buy, and this became a battleground. Body parts? An omission from the marketplace that was questioned by some market fundamentalist purists. What of the existence of a market in favours from government? Measures to prevent the emergence of that market were one of the vital differences between dysfunctional societies, in which it was obligatory to hand over money when stopped by the police, and functional ones, in which the policeman would immediately put you under arrest if you tried. In 1874 a contract to pay a lobbyist to influence Congress was perceived as such an illegitimate purpose that the Supreme Court struck down the attempt by the lobbyist to enforce payment. 'If any of the great corporations of the country were to hire adventurers to procure the passage of a general law with a view to the promotion of their private interests,' Justice Swayne thundered, 'right-minded men would instinctively denounce the employer and employed as steeped in corruption and the employment as infamous.'[5] By 2010, as we shall see in the next chapter, the climate had changed, and so had the view of the Court.

BUSINESS: THE RISE AND FALL OF SHAREHOLDER VALUE

An implication of 'greedy, lazy, selfish' was that leaders, whether in business or politics, faced a problem. They knew what their workforce should do, since they 'knew the model', but since the people they hired lacked any intrinsic motivation but were maximizing only their own self-interest, they would shirk, pilfer or worse. Businesses pioneered and governments increasingly imitated, similar designs: a common approach to motivating their workforce to maximize measurable targets.

How could a CEO get such recalcitrant material as Economic Man to work in the interest of the organization? More economic research – supported with more Nobel Prizes – developed principal-agent theory as the solution: the CEO needed to set up a monitoring system for scrutinizing the behaviour of workers and link it to incentives and penalties that would induce them to do what was wanted. Monitored incentives would entrap employees in a web of scrutiny linked to rewards and penalties.

The financial sector, unsurprisingly, was the most faithful adherent of this 'solution' to the employers' problem: humble bank tellers were given targets for selling products neither they nor their customers understood; and, even now, the bonus season is the high point of the investment banker's year. Law and accountancy abandoned their stuffy professional ethos in search of revenue generation. As an approximate guide, one corporate CEO was worth three top lawyers, seven top accountants and around a hundred and fifty ordinary wage-earners. Acknowledging what they thought had shaped hunter-gatherer societies, a widely adopted payment system is known as 'eat what you kill'. But the advocates of 'eat what you kill' misunderstood those pressures. Real hunter-gatherer societies had learned that by acting cooperatively not only could they reduce the feast/famine of individual hunting by sharing the catch, but that they also caught more. In the time of Adam Smith, Rousseau explained why. Hunters do not 'eat what they kill', because as individual hunters they would only catch hares; by hunting together they can catch stags.[6] So they share their catch, and their social rules confer economic advantage on the group.

How did people reconcile the reality that large business organizations play a central role in modern life with that shrivelled view of society as a forum for transactions between autonomous individuals? In two – largely incompatible – ways. One was to individualize even the largest businesses. Whereas the great pre-war business leaders – such as Alfred Sloan of General Motors or Harry McGowan of ICI – had not been public figures, those of the late twentieth century – Bill Gates and Jack Welch, Lee Iacocca and Richard Branson – would be media stars: in the pages of the business press, GE *was* Welch, Microsoft *was* Gates.

The other approach was to look through the corporation in a reductionist style: the corporation was merely a cypher for the interests of individuals. At a popular level, the business was simply an agency for the individual interests of its shareholders and bore no moral load – 'the social responsibility of business is to maximize its profits', to quote the notorious words of Milton Friedman.[7] At a more academic level, the firm was reduced to a 'nexus of contracts': merely a convenient legal fiction to accommodate a set of private agreements between individual investors, employees, suppliers and customers.

Market fundamentalism predicted that the maximization of shareholder value would be good for society – that only as long as firms strain to maximize profits will the economy be socially efficient. And it is, lest we forget, good for shareholders. Yet it was not good for the person in day-to-day charge of the whole operation – the self-interested CEO. Since the CEO was no more altruistically interested in the business than his workforce, shareholders needed some means of motivating him.

The solution was to incentivize the CEO by the further application of principal-agent theory. Since there was little scope to monitor the details of how the CEO worked, rewards for the CEO might be linked to the value the firm would create for shareholders under his management through the award of share options. Only this would drive the CEO to become totally devoted to the share price. This would set the scene for the explosive growth of CEO remuneration in the next three decades, cheered on by an army of 'remuneration consultants' who devised LTIPs (long-term incentive plans). The 'long term' might extend for as much as three years.

Most people outside business, and many within it, understandably find this characterization of business as motivated only by profit, with individual behaviour driven only by greed, repellent. If that is what business and businesspeople are like, they do not want either business or businesspeople near their schools or hospitals, or their water supply, or perhaps anywhere at all. To the extent that this characterization has been true of businesspeople (and sometimes it has), we entirely agree.

A CASE FOR TREATMENT

The pharmaceutical industry is one of the great successes of modern business. Antibiotics, anti-hypertensives, statins, vaccines and many other products have saved hundreds of millions of lives and improved the quality of life for almost everyone. And made large profits for investors.

George Merck, president from 1925 to 1950 of the pharmaceutical company his family had founded in nineteenth-century Germany, observed that: 'We try never to forget that medicine is for the people. It is not for the profits. The profits follow, and if we have remembered that, they have never failed to appear. The better we have remembered it, the larger they have been.'[8] For many years Merck topped *Fortune* magazine's list of most-admired companies. The company was an exemplar of successful long-term corporate strategy in business guru Jim Collins's 1994 classic *Built to Last*.

Johnson & Johnson's 308-word credo, the work of R. W. Johnson, another member of a founding family, captures similar sentiments to those of George Merck. In a classic business-school case on ethics and corporate reputation, the company's executives applied the credo to implement a speedy product recall of Tylenol, the business's best-selling painkiller, after a maniac spiked containers with cyanide.

The drugs industry had for a long time an implicit contract with public and government. It was permitted extraordinary profitability in return for companies behaving as exemplary corporate citizens. But those days have long gone.

Drug companies came under pressure from Wall Street to demonstrate commitment to shareholder value. The pay-off from marketing is immediate, the pay-off from research delayed, and industry strategy came to reflect that. Merck stumbled – it would feature again in a later book by Collins, *How the Mighty Fall* (2009). The company promoted a new painkiller, Vioxx, not just for the minority of patients who derived a unique benefit but for many who might as advantageously, if less profitably for the pharmaceutical industry, have taken an aspirin.

US law permitted direct advertising of prescription drugs to patients and for a time Vioxx was the most heavily promoted product in that category. Then its use was linked to heart conditions in some patients. Merck withdrew the product amid recrimination and lawsuits. Even the revered Johnson & Johnson would find its reputation tarnished by the regulator's discovery of bad practice – and dubious management responses – at the company's McNeil consumer-products group.

Still, Merck and Johnson & Johnson deservedly remain respected businesses – the latest *Fortune* list put J&J at 26 and Merck at 49 in its top 50 admired companies.[9] But they are now outliers in their industry. When Michael Pearson took over as chief executive of Valeant Pharmaceuticals in 2008, he adopted a new strategy. Others in the industry had been edging towards this approach, but Pearson made it entirely explicit. Valeant bought established drug companies, stopped research and development, emphasized marketing and raised substantially the prices of the proven products to which it had acquired the rights. For a time, the company's profits and share price responded favourably, and Pearson and other executives rewarded themselves accordingly. Some senior employees revelled in the atmosphere of unfettered greed sufficiently thoroughly to commit fraud.[10] When this was revealed, Pearson was forced out and the shares plummeted; the company has since rebranded itself as Bausch Health, taking the name of the respected eyeglass supplier which it had acquired. Valeant's approach found imitators, however. Mylan acquired the rights to EpiPen® – used to provide urgent relief to people with severe allergies – and raised the price sixfold.[11] Martin Shkreli adopted an even more extreme strategy of price gouging at Turing Pharmaceuticals, raising the cost per pill of Daraprim, on the market since 1953, from $13.50 per pill to $750.

But the most egregious abuse was the aggressive marketing of addictive drugs. Purdue Pharmaceuticals, privately owned by the Sackler family, is now notorious for its role in the provision of opioids to small-town America. But even Johnson & Johnson has been fined $572 million for its – relatively minor – role in 'deaths of despair'.[12] The boundaries kept being pushed. Insys had developed an opioid for terminally ill cancer patients, for whom its highly addictive properties were of no consequence. But this market was doubly limited: only the terminally ill were customers, and they soon ceased to be so. The head of sales for Insys, Alec Burlakoff, hired a stripper to persuade physicians to promote and prescribe it to non-terminal patients, giving a new interpretation to the term 'hooker'. Once hooked, such patients were indeed dead profitable. In an interview with the *Financial Times*, Burlakoff acknowledged that he did not have 'morals, ethics and values'.[13] He described his thinking once he realized that prosecution was likely: 'Not only is the company going to get fined an astronomical amount of money, which I've seen a million times, but worse-case scenario, which I've never seen before, they might actually take *my* money.' Burlakoff and his fellow executives were prosecuted under federal racketeering legislation aimed at criminal gangs and are now serving prison terms. A pharmaceutical industry that once seemed to exemplify a constructive relationship between private enterprise and public benefit is now widely and justifiably detested.

But the damage has not been just to the legitimacy of business in the eyes of its customers, but to the businesses themselves. The organization whose purpose is shareholder value has little to offer its employees other than their paychecks. It is hard to imagine that even the most committed chief executive leaps out of bed each morning enthused by the prospect of creating more shareholder value. Valeant, Turing, Purdue and Insys were damaged, mostly beyond repair, by the greed of their own employees.

Institutions designed around the assumption that individuals are selfish and greedy discover that the assumption is self-fulfilling. The people they attract are likely to be selfish and greedy, and, if they are not, they discover that there is only disadvantage to any other style of behaviour. Only the most depraved individual could derive job satisfaction from promoting opioid addiction. And there is not much job satisfaction in selling collateralized debt obligations, or working eighteen hours a day on unimportant errands as a new hire in a law firm or investment bank.

The reductionist accounts of the corporation bore no relationship to the reality of how successful and sustainable modern businesses – such as Johnson & Johnson and Merck – had actually functioned, but the rhetoric was influential. And corrosive: business was ethically contemptible – and unapologetic about it. Reductionist thinking discarded the only basis on which corporate organizations could claim legitimacy in a democratic society – that they delivered the goods and services which people wanted, and provided satisfying and rewarding employment to many. Absent such justification, there is no adequate answer to the question of legitimacy provoked by Friedman's assertion that the social responsibility of business is to extract as much profit as possible from the community – 'why should we allow them to do that?'

METRICS IN GOVERNMENT

If the social responsibility of firms was to maximize profits, perhaps the social responsibility of government was to maximize the sum of incomes – GDP.* The centre-right focussed on sustaining growth. George Osborne – British Chancellor of the Exchequer from 2010 to 2016 – celebrated that austerity and corporate-tax reductions were enabling Britain to have the fastest GDP growth in the G7, a triumph somewhat dented by the challenge from a left-behind northern voter – 'that's *your* GDP.'[14] The centre-left, converted to the merits of the market, also accepted that growth was the objective, so long as all had access to its potential benefits. Consequently, Tony Blair's top three priorities were 'education, education, education'. The route to equality was that everyone should have a chance of joining the meritocracy.

Governments, responsible for public services, appeared to face the same problem as firms. The heads of public-sector organizations knew what their workers should do, but why would a workforce made up of Economic Men do it? Within the framework of received ideas, there was only one solution, and public officials increasingly adopted it. Activities that had remained in the public sector, such as health, education and social care, were usually high in intrinsic motivation, but hard to monitor. But, increasingly, public-sector workers were turned into automata to be monitored and incentivized, rather than people whose judgement could be trusted. Targets were everywhere.

---

* GDP is not in fact the sum of incomes, but it is nearly so, and these technical issues worried few.

Ninety-five per cent of accident-and-emergency cases in Britain were to be seen within four hours (!), 90 per cent of emergency ambulances were to arrive within eight minutes. When the targets were achieved, it was at a cost: stripped of autonomy, workers could easily become demotivated, or game the incentives by diverting their effort only to what was measured.

But perhaps the real need was to motivate the heads of public-sector organizations themselves. There were suggestions that the governor of New Zealand's central bank should receive a bonus determined by how low inflation was.[15] One of us recalls attending a dinner for the heads of eleven European civil services at which Britain's head-of-service proudly explained that not only were monitored incentives being adopted throughout the public sector, but he himself was on an incentive pay system, linked to targets for which the prime minister was his assessor. Perhaps the head of the British civil service worked harder and more effectively than he would have done without the monitored incentives. We doubt it, and we also doubt whether someone who needed to be motivated by such measures would be the right person to head the civil service. When the head of Germany's civil service was asked whether he was on a similar system, his laconic reply was 'Of course not.'

UTILITARIAN INDIVIDUALISM AND THE RISE OF GLOBAL SALVATIONISM

Perhaps governments should maximize not the sum of incomes but the sum of utilities. Utilitarian individualism finds its origin in the thinking of the English philosophers John Stuart Mill and Jeremy Bentham in the nineteenth century. In Bentham's words, 'It is the greatest good to the greatest number of people which is the measure of right and wrong.'[16] Such thinking has been a major strand of ethical thought ever since. The general good is the aggregate of individual goods. *Act utilitarianism* – every action is to be judged by its effect on this general good – is commonly distinguished from *rule utilitarianism* – we seek that social order which would achieve that general good. The lie which has a beneficial consequence is approved by act, but not rule, utilitarianism. And it is rule utilitarianism which has an elective affinity with the economic models described above. Individuals maximize their own utility, and government should maximize the sum of these individual utilities.

But there were some things which everyone agreed the market could not do. Some needs, such as defence, needed public provision. Some people were not in a position to earn a living: how could they be supported? Both public goods and transfers to the needy would have to be financed by taxes, but what should be the extent of such provision and who should pay? To answer these types of question in a world of otherwise autonomous individuals, the government appeared to need a way of summing the preferences of individuals for public goods and transfers. Another post-war literature sought to describe how a 'social welfare function' might be assembled from the aggregate of individual preferences. Somewhat disconcertingly, an 'impossibility theorem' demonstrated that there was no scheme of aggregation which met a set of apparently reasonable conditions.[17]

Whose preferences should be included? To the most assertive of modern utilitarians, Peter Singer, 'It makes no moral difference whether the person I can help is a neighbor's child ten yards from me or a Bengali whose name I shall never know, ten thousand miles away.'[18] Or someone who has not yet been born. The Victorian utilitarian Henry Sidgwick asked, 'How far are we to consider the interests of posterity when they seem to conflict with those of existing human beings? It seems, however, clear that the time at which a man exists cannot affect the value of his happiness from a universal point of view; and that the interests of posterity must concern a Utilitarian as much as the interests of his contemporaries.'[19] For Frank Ramsey, Keynes's great colleague and contemporary, discounting the future was 'a practice which is ethically indefensible and arises merely from the weakness of the imagination'.[20] Singer would go on to suggest that the welfare of animals must also form part of the calculus. The category of present and future beings for whom strict utilitarianism might call on us to make sacrifices becomes infinitely large.

Here was one answer to the question of what government should maximize: the sum of the utilities of all the people who might be born anywhere on the planet at any time in the future. There were, of course, potentially a lot of them. Calculations of this kind were made in all seriousness in reviewing the implications of climate change.

Global salvationism became influential in practical policy-making. No distinction was made between the utility of citizens and non-citizens, and senior civil servants thought that immigration would increase the sum of these utilities. One of us was told by a Treasury official, 'It would be helpful if you said that immigration benefits everyone: of course, it doesn't have to be true.'

David Goodhart describes Britain's most senior civil servant – the one who was himself on incentive pay – explaining that 'I think it's my job to maximize global welfare, not national welfare,' and turning to the Director-General of the BBC, who agreed with him.[21] Yet we doubt if he would have encountered similar agreement among ordinary British citizens. Many people would sympathize with the plight of the Bengali 10,000 miles away, and even make a modest contribution to the relief of famine there; but many of the same people would regard the idea that the neighbour's child had no stronger claim on their concern as risible. And not just people in Britain, but people in Bengal: we all differentiate our obligations to others, giving priority to acknowledged mutuality. We provide help most readily and most generously to our friends and family, and then, more modestly, to our neighbours and to wider circles of people, our sense of obligation diminishing with spatial and temporal distance and the change of category from acknowledged mutuality to unreciprocated altruism. That sense of mutual obligation, not global salvationism, is the prosociality natural to humanity.

And so civil servants and politicians who subscribed to global salvationism faced a problem. Politicians were beholden to voters, and voters cared about themselves and their families and neighbours more than they cared about potential immigrants and the as yet unborn great-grandchildren of the Bengali whose name they would never know. Global salvationism was not something they would vote for. And they would not support policies towards foreign aid, immigration and climate change derived from that assumption.

As ordinary voters began to sense that their governments had ethical priorities that diverged from their own, their trust in government was gradually eroded. If the heads of the civil service and the BBC were happy to sacrifice national welfare for global welfare, if Treasury officials thought it all right to lie for its cause, the subsequent mutinies were unsurprising.

ANNEX: MARKET FUNDAMENTALISM: THE UNDERLYING ECONOMIC MODEL

Since the Second World War, most economic models have been based on assumptions of rational choice by individuals in line with their own individual preferences, a framework set out most fully by Paul Samuelson and extended to choice-under-uncertainty by Friedman and Savage. Such models formed the basis of the framework of efficient competitive market equilibrium described by Arrow and Debreu.[22] This careful mathematical analysis demonstrated that uncoordinated decisions by individuals could nevertheless produce collectively coherent outcomes – a discovery which may be the most profound insight of economics.

Initially, rational choice meant no more than consistency in the application of these preferences – if I choose the steak *au poivre* at my favourite restaurant today, I will choose it again if I return next week. Consistency allows for the possibility of altruism, albeit somewhat fatuously: thus my utility is being maximized by the warm feeling engendered by my generosity. Indeed, since this argument can account for more or less any behaviour, it has little content: even if I choose a different dish at the restaurant, it must be because I have a taste for variety; if I do not send another cheque to the charity, we just learn more about my preferences – specifically, the diminishing marginal returns to my generosity.

Evidently, the claim that what I have done must maximize my utility, otherwise I wouldn't have done it, lacks power to explain what I have done, far less predict what I might do. And so, in practical application, utility maximization came to mean something more specific: that people respond to financial incentives. Enter *possessive individualism*: Economic Man was greedy and selfish. And lazy. Effort reduced his utility.

There was no place in this structure for voluntary cooperative arrangements: all relationships were transactional. But, as Arrow and Hahn had recognized, while the world of selfishness might sound a dispiriting recipe for dystopia, analysis of how such an economy might work came to the opposite conclusion. Economic analysis of selfishness mediated through markets showed that (provided one made enough assumptions, some implausible and some fantastical) individual greed would result in efficient outcomes.

All the productive potential of the economy would be realized, leaving no scope for making anyone better off without someone else being made worse off. Greed was good because it drove people to realize this potential to the maximum. Rational choice premises were employed in the description of the business corporation presented by financial economists such as Jensen and Meckling, and legal scholars such as Easterbrook and Fischel.[23] It is difficult to exaggerate the extent of the influence of this family of models on academic departments of economics and politics over the last fifty years.

Economic Man still had to cope with the uncertainty of a complex world. But there was a fix for this. Everything is either knowable or unknowable. Economic Man knew all that was knowable; thus he would not make systematic errors but hold 'rational expectations'. He 'knew the model'. As Thomas Sargent, one of the developers of this idea, explained, 'There is a communism of models. All agents inside the model, the econometrician, and God share the same model.'[24] Everything that could be known was known by everybody.

Although Economic Man 'knew the model', from time to time he might be derailed by the unknowable: 'shifts' or 'shocks' – as when the dinosaurs were made extinct by the asteroid. Or when banks collapsed in the 2008 global financial crisis. The model worked well except when it didn't, and then one would know that the economy had fallen victim to shifts or shocks. Difficult though it may be for non-economists to believe, Nobel Prizes were awarded for this discovery and similar models are still taught and developed today. And, since everything that was not known was unknowable, not only would we try to maximize fulfilment of our self-interest, we knew how to do it. The model told us that, taken as a whole, these decisions would maximize social welfare. Not only would we be maximizing global welfare, we knew how to do that too. Until the next shock.

The disastrous consequences of 'we know the model' have taught some of its disciples belated humility. 'I made a mistake in presuming that the self-interest of organizations, specifically banks, is such that they were best capable of protecting shareholders and equity in the firms . . . I discovered a flaw in the model that I perceived is the critical functioning structure that defines how the world works.'[25] Thus spoke a penitent Federal Reserve Chairman Alan Greenspan; but a little too late. Still, Greenspan acknowledged error. Others identified the crisis simply as a 'shock' and saw no need for apology for their failure to anticipate the consequences of the explosive growth of trade in poorly understood securitized products. Market fundamentalism was so intellectually hermetic that it even survived the global financial crisis. It was never entirely clear whether its proponents had predicted the crisis or shown that such things could not be predicted, but the consensus seemed to favour the latter.

In essence, the theorems about market efficiency created by the activities of Economic Man explain the conditions under which a society of sociopaths would be able to function. Since these conditions are rarely fulfilled – Arrow and Hahn had correctly observed that we learned from these models the ways in which markets would not work well as well as the ways in which they would – the efficient paradise of competitive equilibrium analysis never existed, and never could. But fortunately, we don't need them to be, since most people are not sociopaths.

3

Rights

> 'The notion of obligations comes before that of rights, which
> is subordinate and relative to the former.'
> – Simone Weil, *The Need for Roots: Prelude to a*
> *Declaration of Duties towards Mankind* (1949;
> English translation 1952)

As the Soviet Union imploded and socialism collapsed – while capitalism persistently failed to do so – the political left found solace in its own modes of individualistic thought. The rising class of the beneficiaries of meritocracy embraced the notions of individual rights and personal identity as they retreated from the language of social solidarity. Politicians and policy-makers across the political spectrum perceived individuals and the state as the principal economic agents: disagreements were over their relative power. Both camps saw the definition and upholding of rights as the primary state function and the scope of such rights as the primary focus of political argument. For one camp, property rights were central; the other attached more weight to human and social rights.

A Theory of Justice by John Rawls, published in 1971, has been the most influential work of political philosophy in the last fifty years. Finding its inspiration in the long-established social-contract theory of Hobbes and Locke, Rawls asked what economic and political arrangements self-interested individuals might agree to if they did not know what position they would occupy in the resulting society. Rawls rejects utilitarianism because it fails to 'take seriously the plurality and distinctness of individuals'.[1] 'Each person possesses an inviolability founded on justice that even the welfare of society as a whole cannot override. For this reason justice denies that the loss of freedom for some is made right by a greater good shared by others.'[2] The world he describes is populated by individuals and the state. Rawls believed that an egalitarian outcome would be supported by individuals who feared that they would find themselves in a disadvantaged role. Awarding Rawls the National Medal for the Arts and Humanities in 1999, President Clinton claimed that the philosopher had 'helped a whole generation of learned Americans revive their faith in democracy'.[3] Rawls appeared to reconcile fairness with individualism, justice with liberty.

If Rawls was the political philosopher of the democratic left, his Harvard colleague Robert Nozick was the political philosopher of the libertarian right. In *Anarchy, State and Utopia*, published in 1974, he argued for the necessary fairness of the free exchange of goods and services among individuals. The economic models described in the previous chapter were interpreted as providing an efficiency argument for market fundamentalism. Nozick now provided a further argument for market fundamentalism based on justice. The combination of fairness in the initial distribution of property rights and voluntary exchange ensures the justice of the market outcome. The high earnings of Wilt Chamberlain (the leading American basketball player at the time Nozick was writing) were just because, given the fair initial distribution, everyone thought it worth contributing for the privilege of seeing Chamberlain score. Nozick explicitly denied any agency beyond the individual: 'There is no *social entity* with a good that undergoes some sacrifice for its own good. There are only individual people, different individual people, with their own lives.'[4] The resonance with Margaret Thatcher's subsequent 'there is no such thing as society' is evident.

Friedman's claim that 'the social responsibility of business is to maximize its profits' rests, perhaps unexpectedly, not on an economic argument that such behaviour would promote the general good through its effect on the efficiency of corporations, but on a moral claim reflecting the alleged property rights of stockholders as owners. Thus market fundamentalism originated in possessive individualism and claimed to derive strength both from utilitarian individualism *and* rights-based individualism. Unfettered markets would not only promote the greatest good of the greatest number, but such a regime – and only such a regime – would protect just entitlement.

THE ORIGINS OF PROPERTY RIGHTS

Nozick's theory of justice is based on historic entitlement, derived from just acquisition, just transfer, by unforced disposition or voluntary exchange, or by restitution, where there has been unjust transfer. But what constitutes 'just acquisition'? On this, Nozick has little to say.

But Rousseau did: 'The first man who, having enclosed a piece of ground, bethought himself of saying "This is mine", and found people simple enough to believe him, was the real founder of civil society. From how many crimes, wars, and murders, from how many horrors and misfortunes might not any one have saved mankind, by pulling up the stakes.'[5] The 'horrors and misfortunes' of possessive individualism.

But in attacking the right to own a farm, Rousseau had not chosen his ground well. Territoriality is not an invention of modern humans and the protection of territorial rights of both individuals and groups is not a novelty of the modern state. Many animals and birds demonstrate such territoriality and defend their 'rights' to territory either individually or collectively. What distinguishes modern economic life is not claims to land, but the variety of economic rights which society has created beyond the territorial. What, beyond physical enclosure, constitutes 'just acquisition'?

The reason Jeff Bezos is the richest man on the planet is that corporate law enables the founder of a business to claim a share of its future revenues, not just now but into the indefinite future, and provides and protects institutions which enable these rights to be sold to investors. There is nothing self-evidently just about these arrangements. But they are the source of the wealth not just of Bezos but of most of the people who appear on the usual lists of the world's wealthiest people: they are business founders such as Bernard Arnault, Mark Zuckerberg; or the children of Sam Walton. The Grosvenor and Cadogan families, whose ancestors had the good fortune to place their stakes around the land which would become Mayfair and Belgravia, are the exception, not the rule.

That description of the origins of wealth is true of Britain and the United States, and of parts of Western Europe and Asia. Less so elsewhere. Large fortunes have been made from the privatization of state-owned assets in former communist states. And there are people who lived on mostly unpromising-looking territory – desert, permafrost, veldt – under which oil or gold or some other valuable resource was discovered by others. Some became rich from the recognition that small percentages of very large sums add up to large sums – the loading charges for coal at Cardiff Docks made the Bute family one of the richest in nineteenth-century Britain; licence fees for the MS-DOS operating system propelled Bill Gates to financial stardom; advice on multibillion-dollar corporate acquisitions enabled investment bankers to retire early in luxury.

Intellectual property now represents another lucrative form of property right, with an almost random distribution of benefit – while MS-DOS was protected by copyright, the graphical user interface was not; anti-ulcer treatments were and remain one of most profitable products of the pharmaceutical industry, however the discovery that many ulcers could be quickly and permanently cured by a high dose of antibiotics generated a Nobel Prize, but little other financial reward, for its contributors. And the value of the trademark 'We' was greater than the financial rewards accruing to the inventor of the theory of relativity, or the people who cracked DNA or invented the internet. Lobbying and litigating around intellectual property has, not surprisingly, become a major business activity in its own right.

Most property rights are social constructs; their design and protection are a primary function of a political system, and their effectiveness key to economic prosperity. Garrett Hardin famously described 'the tragedy of the commons' the days before enclosure, before Rousseau's stakes in the ground, in which the pursuit of unregulated self-interest led to the degradation of common property for all.[6] But Elinor Ostrom deservedly received the Nobel Prize for demonstrating how inventive historical and traditional societies had been in constructing social norms and rules to avert these problems.

Secure and legitimate property rights – and without legitimacy there can be little security – are essential to the functioning of prosperous economies. But there are many possible property-rights regimes, and not all are equal, whether judged by the criteria of justice or those of efficiency. The regime that modern societies have evolved seems to owe more to accidents of history and corporate lobbying than to these more fundamental criteria. A copyright regime which originated in the desire of the state to control seditious literature is not necessarily appropriate for the designers of smartphone apps. And the extension of copyright to seventy years after the death of the author did little to enhance incentives to literary creativity – certainly if our own experience is any guide – but much to enable the Disney Corporation to continue to derive profits from its lucrative Mickey Mouse franchise. There are many possible structures of corporate law, and many ways of organizing financial markets, or awarding mineral royalties. Those who worry about inequalities of income and wealth should devote more attention to these underlying causes of the inequalities they cite.

THE HUMAN RIGHTS REVOLUTION

The UN Declaration of Human Rights was promulgated in the immediate aftermath of the Second World War and was a laudable attempt, enthusiastically promoted by Eleanor Roosevelt, to point towards a better world. It asserts and defines thirty 'fundamental rights'.[7] The first twenty-one are civil and political rights. They are predominantly *negative* rights – such as the right not to be subject to arbitrary detention or arrest. The remaining nine rights are social and economic. Article 25(1) reads: 'Everyone has the right to a standard of living adequate for the health and well-being of himself and of his family, including food, clothing, housing and medical care and necessary social services, and the right to security in the event of unemployment, sickness, disability, widowhood, old age or other lack of livelihood in circumstances beyond his control.' Article 26(1) states: 'Everyone has the right to education. Education shall be free, at least in the elementary and fundamental stages. Elementary education shall be compulsory. Technical and professional education shall be made generally available and higher education shall be equally accessible to all on the basis of merit.'

The influence of this UN Declaration on subsequent policy and philosophy has been large, and not entirely in ways that are desirable or were foreseen at the time. Rights for some have practical meaning only if they impose obligations on others. The civil and political rights in the Declaration are and were intended to be, primarily, *individual* rights against *the state*. The Declaration requires the state to refrain from political censorship and incarceration without due process. But what of the economic rights, the positive rights? If there is a right to free education, who is required to provide – and pay for – that free education? The only answer to this question can be 'the state'. The authors of the Declaration plainly did not intend that I could knock on the door of a friend, far less a stranger, and say that I had come to exercise my right to housing. And if they had so intended, they would quickly have discovered that there was little political support for such a right and that the assertion of the right to shelter undermined the willingness of many people to provide shelter voluntarily to friends in need.

The claim to individual entitlements undermines solidarity; the existence of legal rights – whether or not these rights are effectively honoured – diminishes the force of moral obligation. 'It's the government's job.' 'Why don't social services do something?' Such language hollows out community and hence diminishes the role of agency as exercised by any entities other than individual and state. Yet, historically, many such entities were active in the provision of education, health care, housing and many of the other economic goals listed in the Declaration. Less so today. The state is necessary: it has an important role in meeting social needs. But it should aim to complement, and sometimes regulate, other forms of provision, rather than replace them.

The distinction between human rights and property rights was elided. In *Citizens United* in 2010, the US Supreme Court ruled unconstitutional any restriction on the right of corporations to make political contributions. The right of free speech included the right to sell one's opinion to the highest bidder. And accorded the highest bidder the right to buy it. Perhaps 'one man, one vote' should be 'one dollar, one vote'. There were no longer things money just can't buy, as Justice Swayne had thought in 1874, as The Beatles had sung in the 1960s, and as the moral philosopher Michael Sandel, to whose work we shall return, has continued to argue.

It took the #MeToo movement to reassert common sense. The right not to be sexually harassed was a right not to be sexually harassed. Period. It was not a tradeable property, a right to receive suitable monetary or non-monetary compensation in return for suffering sexual harassment.

RIGHTS TALK

The term 'rights talk' was popularized by legal scholar Mary Ann Glendon. The subtitle of her book of the same name – *The Impoverishment of Political Discourse* – emphasizes another consequence. Perhaps rights are never absolute – as in Justice Oliver Wendell Holmes's famous denial of the right to shout 'Fire!' in a crowded theatre (a case notorious because the court's denial of free speech was far more extensive than that).[8] But even if rights are not absolute, they are intended to establish a strong presumption – rights are trumps, as legal philosopher Ronald Dworkin put it.[9]

But how do we know whether such a right exists? The first declarations of 'natural' rights were made in the American and French revolutions. An underlying problem was quickly evident – the rights of men which were self-evident to Jefferson, Franklin and Adams were not necessarily self-evident to women, King George III or to slaves or slave-owners. Just as Bentham had thought natural rights 'nonsense on stilts', in the modern era Alasdair MacIntyre, to whose thought we shall return, likened belief in natural rights to belief in witches and unicorns.[10] One does not negotiate a right, one asserts it. If the right is denied or disputed, the response is to shout louder – or, as in the American and French revolutions and the American Civil War, to resort to force of arms.

What if rights conflict? The adversarial legal processes of the Anglo-Saxon world are inherently binary. There is a winner and there is a loser: a right either exists or it does not. In the United States, the debate over abortion is polarized between the 'right to life' and the 'right to choose'. Glendon is a conservative Catholic, for whom the 'right to life' is an overriding priority – a position which has appealed to Trump, whose appointment of her as chair of a commission on international human rights angered many American women. But on what basis are conflicting claims to a right, such as a right to life, and a right to choose, to be resolved? On the basis, it would seem, of whoever asserts the right most forcibly. The US abortion debate is one in which competitive shouting has sometimes degenerated further into actual violence. Fifty years after the Supreme Court judgment in *Roe v. Wade* somewhat implausibly deduced a right to *choose* from a discovered right to *privacy*, that debate still rages. Contrast the position in most European countries, where compromises have evolved which command wide public acceptance.

Does the right to bear arms include the right to deploy an automatic rifle? To what extent is a right to freedom of speech a right enforceable against private entities such as the *Daily Mail*, universities, Facebook and Twitter? How can the right to freedom from arbitrary detention be reconciled with the need to protect the public from radicalized individuals with malevolent intentions? When is arrest or detention *arbitrary*? All of these are questions which cannot be answered without reference to their practical context. All of them are questions about which there may be legitimate disagreement, both as to what the consequences are and as to what conclusions should be drawn from them. And all of them are questions on which a democratic society should seek, and can reasonably hope to find, a substantial measure of agreement which is unlikely to be fully satisfactory to anyone. But the stridency of extreme individualism has made such a process of negotiation and mediation difficult to manage.

4

From Civil Rights to Expressive Identity

*'We are CEOs of our own companies. Me Inc . . . our most
important job is to be head marketer for the brand called You.'*
                              – Tom Peters, Fast Company, 1997

The civil rights movement which gripped the post-war United States
was a demand for recognition of common citizenship. The oratory
of Martin Luther King, the bravery of many individuals, black and
white, who defied abusive authority, and the political skills of Lyndon
Johnson, produced a revolution in US society. While it by no means
ended racism, it culminated in the election of the United States' first
black president in 2008. There could be no more conclusive demonstration that all Americans were citizens. The movement was the final
act in the process of building the US community, not the opening act
for individualism.

But that community was under pressure from many other individual developments. In a remarkable and widely quoted passage in
Planned Parenthood v. *Casey*,[1] US Supreme Court Justice Anthony
Kennedy asserted that 'At the heart of liberty is the right to define
one's own concept of existence, of meaning, of the universe, and of
the mystery of human life.' This sentiment has a superficial attraction.
But it is the antithesis of membership of a community, a repudiation of
the notion that individuals derive their identity within the context of
the society in which they live: the 'thick culture' described by Michael
Walzer;[2] the 'embedded self' of Michael Sandel – thinkers and concepts to which we shall return.

In 1963, the political philosopher Kenneth Minogue coined the metaphor 'St George in retirement'.[3] The saint, having slain the fearsome dragon which demanded human sacrifices and endangered the life of the young princess, decided he would not lay down his sword but went instead in search of lesser and lesser dragons to slay. Minogue presciently anticipated the consequences of the initial successes of the mutuality of the post-war era in establishing a commonality of citizenship.

In particular, the success of the civil rights campaign then served as a model for proponents of successive waves of social liberalism – for feminists, campaigners for the disabled, gays and lesbians. The language of rights was at the centre of their claims. Yet the analogy was plainly stretched. These social movements sought to redefine traditional gender roles, to secure better access to facilities for disabled people, to establish general acceptance of varieties of sexual preference. They had wholly admirable objectives – but to frame their achievement in the language of rights implied an inappropriate stridency which undermined the ethos of solidarity.

African Americans were citizens whose fundamental rights of citizenship had been suppressed: the rights they sought were intrinsic to their status as citizens. In contrast, when we help a blind person board a train, we do so not because that person has a right and we have a corresponding obligation, but because we are doing what any decent person would do (and we know, but this is not our explicit reason for the act, that if we were blind, most of our fellow citizens would do the same for us). And if the blind person were to stand on the platform asserting his rights, we suspect we would respond rather differently.

CONFLICTING CLAIMS TO RIGHTS

St George claimed the lives of many more dragons as the twentieth century moved into the twenty-first. The addition of letters to the LGBTQ alphabet ended with a + to express the possibility of many further claims to rights. But, as we have noted, rights talk encounters difficulties in the face of competing assertions of incompatible rights.

It seems hard to believe today, but from 1974 to 1984 the Paedophile

Information Exchange (PIE) advertised openly in the UK, and proclaimed the 'right' of children to have sex, including with much older men. The PIE was affiliated to the National Council for Civil Liberties, along with other organizations campaigning for socially liberal causes. Like almost everyone in 2020, we detest paedophilia. We deny the 'right' of children to have sex because we are aware of the overwhelming evidence of the damaging effects of sexual abuse of young people on their long-term mental health, and because of the inability of children meaningfully to consent to adults bent on persuasion for their own gratification.

Today's battleground is one on which, for example, the claimed rights of women appear incompatible with the claimed rights of transgender persons. Almost nothing about this debate lends itself to the dialectic of rights. The same reasoning that justifies scepticism about the 'right' of young children to consent to sex justifies scepticism about the 'right' of young children to choose their gender identity. As we note later, almost all societies have some formal ritual to mark the moment at which adolescents are judged fit to acquire the rights and obligations of adult citizens.

Mermaids, a charity, asserts that 'Under the 2010 Equality Act, any young person has a right to be addressed as their true gender regardless of any diagnosis or medical intervention and irrespective of age. *Mermaids* can assist your school to assist with a child's gender transition.'[4] True gender appears to mean whatever a child wants it to be. We do not doubt that there are situations in which children should be helped to change gender, and it is conceivable that in some of them Mermaids' experience might be useful. But, to take only one example, Paul has a young daughter who recently went through a phase of insisting on wearing boy's clothes at school – something to which her parents readily agreed. But she continued with the typical preoccupations of a girl at home, and has now reverted to a skirt at school. All futures are subject to radical uncertainty: who knows what she will want at eighteen? But we feel she was fortunate that no teacher encouraged her to seek the advice of Mermaids. Difficult judgements about the treatment, if any, of gender dysphoria – the claim to a gender identity different from biological gender – ought to be derived from evidence on the long-term effects on physical and mental health of subjects of medical intervention, and at an age at which young people are judged to be competent to judge about other important matters, not on competing claims about 'rights'.

'Rights talk' impoverishes political discourse because it favours stridency over pragmatism and compromise. It suggests that the way to promote a goal, whether economic or social, is to 'discover' a 'right' to it. Many people and groups have discovered such 'rights' in recent decades. It is absurd that the Supreme Court of the United States should be asked to pronounce on whether a Christian baker who refused to decorate a cake for a gay wedding was exercising his right to religious freedom, or denying the couple's right to be free of discrimination based on sexual preference, with the right to freedom of speech involved as well. The Court chose not to resolve any of these issues but ruled in favour of the baker on narrow procedural grounds, with the result that the very similar case of Baronelle Stutzman, a florist who declined to arrange the flowers for another same-sex wedding, will also engage America's finest legal minds.

And – this is the key point – the very existence of such a court case – here pitching the Alliance Defending Freedom against the American Civil Liberties Union – is symptomatic of a society so polarized between views held as absolutes that provoking a legal dispute is seen as an appropriate means of advancing a cause. Why couldn't the baker just bake the cake? Or the couple just buy their cake from another baker? We look to a society in which people recognize their common citizenship and sort out trivial disputes without resort to the courts.

ACTIVISM

In September 2011 a group of protestors set up tents in Zuccotti Park, in Lower Manhattan, not far from Wall Street. The Occupy movement spread around the world. In London, activists tried to blockade the Stock Exchange but were diverted by police and settled in the nearby St Paul's Churchyard.

At the time, John was writing a government report on aspects of financial services and planning a book on that industry. After a morning spent at the Stock Exchange he thought it appropriate to offer similar time to the protestors and went for a walk through the tented village. There was a lively spirit, and obvious anger. And in the aftermath of the 2008 global financial crisis there was a lot to be justifiably angry about.

But his attempt to get beyond expressions of outrage to specific demands and proposals got nowhere. When he asked what the demonstrators thought about live issues – such as plans to ringfence the retail activities of banks, or the decline of markets in listed securities in favour of private equity, he encountered only bewilderment. Above one tent fluttered a banner saying 'Ban high-frequency trading', and John went towards it, expecting to find someone with some knowledge or understanding of the industry, only to be told that the author of the sign was not around but might arrive later in the day.

Early in the protest, the London campaign had issued an 'initial statement' – 'The current system is unsustainable. It is undemocratic and unjust. We need alternatives; this is where we work towards them.'⁵ But the process of 'working towards them' had plainly not happened. The occupation was performative; the purpose of the protest was to protest. The New York police cleared Zuccotti Park in November 2011; the City of London police emptied St Paul's churchyard early in 2012.

The slogan of Occupy was 'We are the 99%', emphasizing the contrast between the 1 per cent who had profited from the growth of the financial sector and the massive increases in the remuneration of corporate executives, and the rest of the population. But while the demonstrators were not drawn from the 1 per cent, they were hardly representative of the 99 per cent either. A survey of the New York demonstrators showed that they were disproportionately white, male, well educated and affluent.⁶ They were not people whose houses had been foreclosed or who had lost their jobs as a result of the crisis and the bail-outs.

Occupy fizzled out. But it set the stage for a new kind of activism which characterized the decade that followed, which would propel Bernie Sanders and Jeremy Corbyn to prominence and would later in the decade lead to Extinction Rebellion. It was an activism in which intensity of feeling was more important than actual knowledge.

Well before Extinction Rebellion, activists had embraced the environment. Germany's Greens have become a potent threat to the two mainstream parties, which have desperately tried to pre-empt them with concessions. The Japanese tsunami engulfed a foolishly located nuclear power station and caused massive damage. Immediately, the Greens rocketed in the German opinion polls. Germany was at no risk of a tsunami and its nuclear power stations were maintained with typical German thoroughness. Chancellor Merkel, herself a scientist, chose to placate the Greens by announcing the closure of all Germany's nuclear power. Germany still needed the electricity and derives much of it from brown coal, the most carbon-intensive and polluting source of energy. Germany opened its latest coal mine in February 2020 and emits more carbon per head than almost any other country in Europe.[7] The citizens of Germany are not one whit safer than before they closed the nuclear industry, but the additional carbon that Germany is emitting will have real consequences for Africa. There, the effects of climate change are already all too apparent, and its people are ill equipped to cope with it. The activism of the Green Party mitigated an imagined risk that it inflated into prominence, at the expense of aggravating an all-too-real risk facing a billion Africans.

SELF-RIGHTEOUS NARCISSISM

Thus the modern activist who 'feels the Bern' does not, whatever the label might suggest, *do* something to solve social problems. This is not a new phenomenon. One of Dickens's most memorable caricatures is Mrs Jellyby, who features in *Bleak House*. Mrs Jellyby engages in what the novelist calls telescopic philanthropy – she loves humanity in general but not in particular. She neglects her family, takes no interest in the injured child at her door, but spends her days petitioning on behalf of the natives of Borrioboola-Gha, on the left bank of the Niger. The principal, indeed the only, benefit of Mrs Jellyby's activity was the warm glow of self-satisfaction it created in Mrs Jellyby herself. Fending off representatives of other causes, she 'sat smiling at the limited vision that could see anything but Borrioboola-Gha'. Paul has spent

much of his life working to help Africa to catch up with richer societies, and has urged the fortunate people in those rich societies to do
more. But not as more Mrs Jellybys: we need practical measures, such
as curbing the London law firms registering shell companies whose
secrecy facilitates corruption.

Potential candidates for elevation to the status of modern Mrs
Jellyby abound. Hollywood celebrities have discovered that linking
their names to a woke cause heightens their appeal to their youth-
dominated audiences. Since it is commercially advantageous, there is
now a profession of consultants to advise celebrities as to which cause
would be best suited to their marketing of self. And so inevitably, as
the issue of gender dysphoria became woke, it attracted the celebs.
Sure enough, on the BBC's 2020 *New Year Special*, two American
Hollywood celebrities chose Mermaids for the £5,000 that the BBC
offered to whichever charity they chose. Since this was funded out of
the licence fee, which is a fixed amount per household, it was paid for
predominantly by the families of provincial Britain.

The causes chosen by celebrities are directed to what will enhance
their esteem in the eyes of their youthful audiences, rather than the
needs of the communities around them. They arrive on private jets to
warn of climate change and agitate to protect orang-utans in Suma-
tra. Worthwhile causes indeed. But deaths of despair have rocketed
across the United States. And the state in which Hollywood is located
has become the epicentre of disgrace: one of the US's wealthiest states,
it has a major problem of homelessness, lamentable public schooling
and very high rates of incarceration, mostly of minorities. California
is the state of Proposition 13, the infamous law that has prevented
the explosion in property prices from financing the state budget. But
changing these things is not woke.

Mrs Jellyby belatedly discovered that the King of Borrioboola-Gha
has sold her protégés into slavery. Like hers, modern activism is not
based on familiarity with the subjects of the activism, whether these
subjects are the malfeasance of the finance sector, climate change or
the health of transgender children. Contributions to public debate
should be weighted by the quality of the argument rather than the
vehemence and demonstrativeness of expression.

CONSTRUCTIVE ACTIVISM

The great protest movements of the past – the Chartists, the suffra-gettes, participants in the Veterans' March, the civil rights movement – were conducted by people venting complaints about injustices directly suffered by *them*. The new activist causes are more abstract and their demands framed only in the most general of terms. At their worst, they are no more than performative opportunities to display the emoting self.

In contrast to Mrs Jellyby, in Dickens's era more constructively public-spirited people devoted time to work in the community, formed local companies to bring gaslighting and sanitation to towns and cit-ies, and built affordable housing, sometimes for their own employees, and sometimes for a wider community. Sir Titus Salt, Bradford's big-gest mill-owner and the city's member of parliament and mayor gave away his entire fortune for practical benefits to others. In 1849, while he was mayor, cholera struck the city: his workers and citizens were dying en masse. For him, the experience may have been a triggering event, perhaps analogous to the letter received by Bill Gates from his cancer-stricken mother on the great responsibilities of those who had been blessed by great good fortune. Salt's practical philanthropy included pioneering decent housing for his workforce – the town of Saltaire, now a World Heritage Centre. As with the best entrepre-neurship, Salt identified a solution to distress that was sufficiently profitable to be sustainable. Bill and Melinda Gates's science-informed efforts to eradicate malaria are the modern version of a long tradition.

Other public-spirited people worked to build coalitions of support for realistic policy proposals – the means by which William Wilberforce and his associates secured abolition of the slave trade in 1807. Over the next fifity years, the Earl of Shaftesbury successfully promoted reforms to end slavery altogether, to improve the treatment of the mentally ill, and restrict the employment of child labour. In the 1960s, a group of parliamentarians, with the support of Home Secretary Roy Jenkins, secured a series of social reforms, abolishing the death penalty and ending the criminalization of abortion and homosexuality.

But you do not have to be Titus Salt, Shaftesbury or Bill Gates to engage in constructive activism. There is an astonishing capacity within every community for such initiatives, and there are already many thousands of them. Writing this, Paul recalls a long-deceased aunt, who in midlife lost her husband. Finding widowhood hard, she used her sympathetic imagination to see that many other widowed people felt the same. She established a 'Minus-One Club': a name, a venue and a time. It flourished: widowed people found that instead of a choice between loneliness and the asymmetry of invitations from couples, they could make new friends on the basis of shared experience. Years later, a local vicar wrote to thank her for the enormous good she had done. This modest recognition meant a lot to her, not through pride but reassurance: as she aged, it affirmed that she had been 'deserving of love' (even though she herself never again found it).

Wendy Kopp was an undergraduate at Princeton in 1988. As she describes it, 'something seemed wrong to me about that "Me Generation" label. Most of the people I knew weren't heading to these two-year programs [with investment banks or consulting firms] because they were dead set on making money.'[8] She compared her own schooling in the affluent Dallas suburb of Highland Park with the experience of some of her classmates from less-favoured public schools who struggled to meet Princeton's expectations. So she wrote a senior thesis describing a scheme, modelled on the Peace Corps, under which top graduates would spend two years teaching in disadvantaged schools around the country.

Enthused, Kopp set out to raise funding and after receiving small contributions from Union Carbide and Mobil her persistent letters to Dallas billionaire Ross Perot secured a meeting. Kopp left Perot's office with a cheque for $500,000 and the result was Teach for America, which has sent more than 50,000 young graduates to schools across the US.

Teach for America was the inspiration for Teach First, which has been one factor behind the recent striking improvement in the performance of inner-London schools, and has now been imitated in forty countries.[*] Now Teach, the inspiration of former *Financial Times* columnist Lucy Kellaway, famous for deflating the pretensions of

---

[*] Though not Scotland, where the teachers unions successfully beat off the threat.

management speak, enables people like her who have made successful careers in other fields to end their working lives by returning to school.

And even in London, the epicentre of rampant individualism, where, as you will see, the country's highest income is juxtaposed with the country's highest anxiety and lowest well-being, the natural empathy among families has inspired constructive activism. Little Village harnesses that empathy to connect families with the purpose of ensuring that no child grows up without essential items of clothing, toys and equipment, especially during times of need. Powered by 400 volunteers, many themselves parents with small children, its activists collect donations of clothes, toys and kit for babies and children under the age of five and distribute them to local families who are dealing with challenging circumstances – such as homelessness, unemployment, low wages and domestic violence. Families are introduced to the scheme partly by professionals – such as health visitors and midwives – and partly by faith organizations, other charities and other families. Through reaching out to families, Little Village is helping to build connection and community at the same time as alleviating material poverty. With several hubs across the city, families are welcomed in to choose the items they need while their children play.*

DO THE INDIVIDUALIST ROUTES TO FULFILMENT WORK?

Individualism takes different forms, each proposing a distinctive route to personal fulfilment, but each about 'me'. The first route, and the most mundane, is my consumption, and this is indeed how the economic models see us: we want to consume. But for most successful people the embrace of meritocracy has long replaced consumption: we are fulfilled by our own success. This in turn is now being challenged by the allure of self-expression: I am unique!

Research on well-being casts doubt on each of these routes to fulfilment. Above a modest level, consumption gives only a sugar-rush,

* We would like to thank Lisa Harker of the Nuffield Foundation for telling us about Little Village.

exemplified by the sad evidence from lottery winners.[9] For career success, the news is worse: beyond the £60,000 level, more money actually appears to *reduce* well-being.[10] One recent British survey finds that those earning more than £100,000 a year are *less* satisfied with their lives than the rest of the population.[11] In case that threshold is too low, how about partners in top US law firms, who typically enjoy seven-figure incomes? Well, the depression rate is a wholly exceptional 30 per cent, and drug addiction is rife.[12]

Which leaves the self-realization of expressive individualism. Historically, the end of adolescence was marked by admission into the community. The young men of Athens took the Ephebic oath in full armour before their induction as citizens. In modern times, Neil MacGregor describes the 'rite of passage': how youth are initiated into their role within society.[13] In Vanuatu, children grow their hair, and, as they are mentored, knots are added to mark their accumulation of understanding: cutting it off marks their rite of passage. The daughters of upper-class English families were introduced to 'Society' at debutante balls. Often these ceremonies were religious – the Jewish bar mitzvah and the Anglican confirmation. Military academies had 'hazing' ceremonies, Mafia 'families' initiations.

But, as MacGregor notes, the rise of individualism critiques the notion of the acquired wisdom of the community. Britain has imported the school prom, which celebrates the release from, rather than the entry into, community ties. Now we are embarked on the radical cultural experiment of self-invention: youths initiate each other into adult worlds of their own. But no child can devise the narrative of their own Torah embroidery, or bind the knowledge they need into their own hair. Self-realization amounts to 'do-it-yourself' realization. The results as measured by youth fulfilment are concerning. Since self-realization gripped the culture, teenage depression has leapt, as has its most severe and measurable manifestation, suicide.[*]

---

[*] In the USA there was a 40 per cent increase in suicide between 2000 and 2017 (National Center of Health Statistics (2018)), and major depression increased by 52 per cent between 2005 and 2017 (J. M. Twenge et al. (2019)). In Britain, in the age range 15–19 the rate of suicide increased by 40 per cent between 1981 and 2018 (the longest series available from the Office for National Statistics ((3 Sept. 2019), Table 8).

Like an overhyped product, individualism looks wonderful until you try it. Titus Salt and Wendy Kopp point the way to something better. We will return to that in Part III. But, first, we turn to the consequences of the rise of individualism and activism for the state and politics.

PART II
Government: Symptoms
of Distress

5

The Rise and Fall of the
Paternal State

*'Public monopoly nationalisation no longer seems the pana-
cea that it used to.'*
— Tony Crosland, *The Future of Socialism*, 1956

The Second World War had bequeathed to Britain a confident state.
The war had built national solidarity, and the state had managed a
planned economy in pursuit of a single shared purpose – Victory! It
was easy to believe that, in combination, the new national solidarity
and state economic direction could transform society, delivering welfare for all and sustained economic growth. The statist emphasis in
post-war politics was a wholly understandable response.

But, due initially to these exaggerated hopes for central planning, and subsequently to the rise of individualism, the state became
overburdened. Central planning, which had been effective at rapidly mobilizing resources to fight a war, was incapable of meeting
the increasingly complex and changing demands of a modern society.
This incapacity was very obvious in the Soviet Empire, which could
build a hydrogen bomb and put a man into space but could not produce cars of quality, or foster pharmaceutical innovations, or invent
personal computers. The state was straying into tasks it could not
do well. As the state started to fail in its new purposes, the solidarity
that had been built during the war was gradually dissipated: people
tend not to identify with failure. The emergence of a rights culture
festooned society with a wide variety of new entitlements, and, since
individuals and groups were shorn of obligations, the state became
their residual legatee. Yet, as demands on the state were increasingly

taking it into functions unsuited to centralization, with the consequent demotivation of failure, the weakening of national solidarity concomitant on the rise of individualism reduced support for the state. US politicians pointed to 'welfare queens', and in 2014 *Benefits Street*, which described a location in Birmingham in which most residents lived on benefits, was the most-watched series on Channel Four television. Taxpayers became less willing to share burdens. And, as the state became frustrated at its inability to deliver complex tasks successfully, it adopted the techniques appropriate for Economic Man, which did little to re-establish it in public esteem.

The consequent inability of the state to meet the high expectations placed on it weakened trust in government, a process common to all the major Western democracies. If the objectives of politicians and senior officials were a combination of global salvationism and the desire to achieve or retain high office, their preoccupations had little connection to the lives and interests of their voters and citizens.

NATIONALIZATION

Today people use the words 'nationalization' and 'privatization' as if they were opposites, but this language conflates two distinct issues – ownership and centralization.

Nationalization under the post-war Labour government meant centralization under Whitehall – legislation established a National Health Service, a National Coal Board, the National Insurance Fund, National Assistance and a Central Electricity Authority. A British Transport Commission not only consolidated the four privately owned rail companies but owned and managed road haulage and long-distance coach services. Nationalization did not just bring private mining companies into centralized state control: *it imposed the same centralized control on entities that were already socially owned* – municipally owned gas and electricity businesses, charitable trusts running hospitals and friendly societies – sometimes run by trade unions – which had been providing welfare. Nationalization was less a critique of private enterprise as ill motivated than a suspicion of *any* activity that lacked centralized coordination. The architect of much of this programme was Herbert Morrison, whose reputation had been built by merging London's multiple local bus and underground rail systems, already mostly publicly controlled, into a unified London Transport.

Morrison extrapolated from his experience in London, and the successes of the planned war economy, to a general presumption that centralization enhanced efficiency. But neither he nor others understood that such contexts are atypical. For Morrison – as for most politicians of the left who achieved office – the objective of the Labour Party's Clause IV – 'to secure for the workers by hand or by brain the full fruits of their industry and the most equitable distribution thereof that may be possible upon the basis of the common ownership of the means of production, distribution and exchange' – was equated with *centralized state control*. But as Crosland, Labour's most thoughtful strategist, had quickly realized, this faith in government monopoly proved unwarranted. The advantages of central coordination which enable you to change easily from the Bakerloo to the Central line or to establish a national grid which allows electricity to be generated throughout the day from the lowest-cost power stations in the country (both measures which had been implemented before 1939) do not extend to controlling every coal mine, steel mill or hospital in the country from the same headquarters. Only a few industries are characterized by the network effects which benefit from monopoly.

The greatest success of Britain's nationalized industries was probably the construction in the 1960s of a national gas grid – a new network – which enabled gas from the North Sea to power central heating in most British homes. But there are few other bright spots.

The planned economy began with farce. The Groundnuts Scheme was a well-intentioned plan to feed post-war Britain and earn foreign currency through a large mechanized project in Africa to produce vegetable oils. Former soldiers were recruited to the 'groundnuts army'. Reports from the field soon revealed the impracticality of the scheme, but politicians in London suppressed them, doubling down on the plan until ignominious failure could no longer be hidden.[1] This fiasco exposed from the beginning what would prove to be repeated weaknesses of state economic management – inappropriate scale instead of limited experiment, followed by unwillingness to hear bad news or learn from it. Both pluralism and discipline were absent.

Public corporations were initially established with considerable financial autonomy, including borrowing powers. The Morrisonian conception of the public corporation had high expectations of its officers – they were to be, in Morrison's phrase, 'high custodians of the public interest'.[2] But the nationalized rail industry, in particular, quickly proved to be a sink for public money. Railways had been overused and under-maintained during the war. More and more households acquired cars, while trucking on an improving road system, stimulated by containerization, took freight away from the rail system. The British Transport Commission's response was to propose an ambitious 'modernization' programme, costed in 1955 at £1.2 billion (around £30 billion at current prices).[3]

As losses accumulated, the Treasury took more and more direct control of the finances of this and other nationalized industries. An ICI executive, Richard Beeching, was appointed Chairman of the new British Railways Board and implemented a sweeping programme of cuts, eliminating many branch lines which attracted only a handful of passengers. To this day, his name is anathema to the substantial fraternity of rail enthusiasts. But usage across the surviving network continued to decline, until the trend was sharply reversed after 1995, coincident with a rail privatization more unpopular even than the much-reviled nationalized industry which preceded it.[*]

But nothing matches the scale of waste in electricity production. Generation capacity had proved inadequate in the exceptionally cold winter of 1963, and a massive programme of investment in electricity fitted the agenda of the Labour government elected the following year, which promised benefits from 'the white heat of technology'. The programme included several giant 2000MW coal-fired stations – throughout our careers in Oxford, every train journey to London

---

[*] The reversal is not wholly attributable to privatization, since the decline also halted in other European countries; but the British case stands out for the scale of recovery in rail utilization.

passed the one at Didcot, an eyesore visible throughout a large area of attractive countryside. But the greatest folly was the ordering of five (later raised to seven) gas-cooled nuclear power stations (AGRs) built to a distinctively British design, amid high expectations for their export potential. There were no exports and it would be more than two decades before the stations worked to plan. Ultimately, the plants were sold for a fraction of their cost to the French nationalized electricity supplier EDF with the government assuming decommissioning liabilities. Much of the new capacity never worked properly, but it didn't really matter because it wasn't really needed. Demand grew less than predicted. And – in behaviour which became a pattern – only piecemeal and decades later did this truth emerge. Again, there had been neither pluralism nor discipline.

Coal, historically the subject of contentious industrial relations – notably the 1926 dispute which led to the General Strike of that year – was the iconic nationalized industry. But industrial relations remained a flashpoint. The militant Arthur Scargill led strikes in the winters of 1971–2 and 1973–4, the latter bringing down Edward Heath's Conservative government and setting the scene for the ascent of Margaret Thatcher as leader of a party determined to break the power of public sector trade unions. In 1984–5 a well-planned government resistance achieved precisely that outcome in the mining industry. The British coal industry effectively closed in the following decade as gas was substituted for coal in power stations as well as homes.

Contrary to widespread popular belief, privatization had not been a major part of the Thatcher government's early plans. The watershed came in 1984, after her second electoral victory. The telephone network required a major programme of investment in digital switching, which made demands incompatible with the government's macroeconomic strategy for public borrowing. The idea of selling a 50 per cent stake in the company originated not as an ideology, but as a wheeze to enable borrowing for such investment to be taken off the government balance sheet. But underpricing of the shares and an extensive advertising campaign had the outcome that the share sale was wildly popular, at least with a – mostly Conservative-supporting – section of the public. And the prospect of much higher pay and freedom from Whitehall control aroused the enthusiasm of initially sceptical public sector managers. Over the following decade, privatization was extended to much of the formerly state-controlled industrial sector, including some activities – such as water and rail – for which this form of organization was clearly less appropriate. By the end of the eighteen years of Conservative government in 1997, the era of the Morrisonian public corporation was also more or less at an end.

GOVERNMENT AND INDUSTRY

Following the nationalizations of the Attlee post-war years, the Labour governments of the 1960s and 1970s established first the Industrial Reorganization Corporation (IRC) and then the somewhat oxymoronic National Enterprise Board. The three flagship achievements of the IRC were the merger of all major surviving car companies into British Leyland; the absorption of all British computer interests into ICL; and the consolidation of the major electrical companies into the General Electric Company (GEC). The answer to industrial problems was scale.

How did these three mega-corporations fare? The car flagship, British Leyland, collapsed in 1974, was then nationalized and eventually broken up. The computing flagship, ICL, collapsed in 1981 and was gradually absorbed into the Japanese manufacturer Fujitsu. The electrical flagship, GEC, collapsed in 2001.

The National Enterprise Board was hardly more effective. Alongside an unsuccessful investment and expansion plan for British Leyland, it promoted national champions in machine tools (Alfred Herbert, failed 1983), semiconductors (Inmos, sold in 1989 to STMicroelectronics, which was jointly owned by the French and Italian governments) and consumer electronics (Sinclair Radionics, failed 1980). Only Rolls-Royce, which had been taken into public ownership in 1971 following the company's crippling cost overruns in its RB 211 engine, survived as a successful company, with its iconic automobile brand now owned by BMW and the (subsequently privatized) aero-engine division one of the three dominant global producers.

None of this is to suggest that government has no useful role in the promotion of industry and innovation, and we will return to the question of what that role should be. But experience of the consolidation of business activities by the British government into national monoliths, whether privately or publicly owned, makes clear what it should *not* be. The saga of overambitious plans, implemented on a large scale, followed by unwillingness to acknowledge, far less reveal, their failure is one which has been repeated over and over again.

HEALTH CARE

A saga repeated even in the jewel in the crown of the Attlee government's legacy: the national provision of health care. In 2002, the New Labour government launched a massive plan to centralize all medical records in a single IT system. Planned as the world's largest IT system, the programme was costed at £2.3 billion.[4] Once again, the plan was too ambitious and the feedback on its progress disingenuous. By 2006, twenty-three computer scientists wrote a public letter warning of failure and complaining that the evidence of that failure was being suppressed; by 2009, a parliamentary committee was warning of huge cost overruns, by then estimated at £12 billion.[5] The programme was gradually wound down, and finally cancelled in 2013.

But this instinct for over-centralization remains strong. During the onset of the coronavirus crisis, the public-policy instinct was again to centralize. Britain was one of the first countries to develop a test, but all testing was centralized at a facility at Colindale in north-west London, itself managed by Public Health England (not the National Health Service England, but itself a national monopoly). As an academic scientist commented, 'If I'm running a lab where every sample of a really interesting new disease has to come to me for testing, then I am in control of the data. In that situation it's a bit difficult to think, "It doesn't matter where the tests are done as long as all the data comes together."'[6] Colindale was reluctant to let other labs, in universities and private firms, test because, for scientists, the best test is one they know to be completely accurate, and this is demanding. As we write, universities capable of and willing to do mass tests in their localities are still being forbidden to do so. Yet, for public policy, what mattered was speed and scale: false positives were less important than false negatives. Britain has belatedly ramped up testing capacity to around 125,000 people weekly, but Germany has already been testing around 500,000 people a week and plans to triple it. Christian Drosten, head of the laboratory that developed Germany's first test, explained: 'We have a culture here in Germany that is not supporting a centralized diagnostic system. So Germany does not have a public health laboratory that would restrict other labs from doing the tests.'[7] Britain's repeated over-centralization of health care is sometimes not only expensive, as with IT, but dangerous.

During the coronavirus crisis, millions of us stood on our doorsteps banging pots to thank NHS workers for their efforts. The ideal of a universal public service free at the point of need appeals to the authors as much as it does to most of our fellow citizens. We need a good system for the national provision of health care, anchored on qualified and purpose-driven workers, but it is not at all obvious that centralizing its running in one massive organization is the best way of achieving it. The organization's gigantic IT system would have been the largest in the world: it didn't work. The organization's monopoly of testing at Colindale didn't produce the world's finest system: it was overwhelmed.

These problems are symptomatic: the diagnosis is not obscure. Britain's health-care organization is the world's third largest employer, behind only Walmart and China's People's Liberation Army. Within our one monopoly health organization are trapped many thousands of dedicated people, with the skills and motivation ideally suited for devolved power of decision. Instead, like social workers, their time is diverted into the form-filling demanded by top-down monitoring. Health care is well suited to decentralized provision, and there is no inconsistency between decentralization and universal access, which is achieved in almost all developed countries (if not in the largest one) through both cooperation and competition bounded by disciplined pluralism. Our monopoly health-care organization is a legacy of Britain's post-war obsession with over-centralization. Not only health care, but the management of local services and industrial policy, have been centralized in Whitehall. The record of failures is now sufficiently persistent that it is time to wake up to it.

HIGHER EDUCATION

The nationalization of universities was a gradual but steady process across the fifty years that followed the Second World War. Oxford and Cambridge and the four old Scottish universities had existed for centuries; but John Owens, a Manchester industrialist, was the first person to recognize in tangible fashion the contribution which a university could make to the community and business of the surrounding city. Owens College opened in 1851, and by the end of the century cities around England were following this example. All these new institutions were, like Manchester, the result of initiatives by local businesspeople. Joseph Chamberlain, whose Nettlefold business had a near-monopoly of screw manufacture in England, and who then embarked on a political career, which his son Neville followed, established the University of Birmingham. The Wills family, tobacco magnates, did the same in Bristol. The University of Sheffield had been founded in 1905: Mark Firth, a local steel magnate, had financed its main building, and the university had naturally excelled in disciplines pertinent to the local economy. The University of Nottingham was founded in 1948 with the aid of Jesse Boot of the eponymous chemist's.

The industrialists of Stoke-on-Trent had never seen the need for higher education, but after the Second World War the local Labour council took a different view. It provided funding and, with the aid of A. D. Lindsay, the Master of Balliol College, Oxford, the University College of North Staffordshire was established. Significantly, the new university was built not in grimy Stoke but on the leafy Keele estate five miles away.

Government funding of universities had begun at the time of the expansion of higher education to cities before the First World War, but most income continued to be derived from fees, endowments and the local community. In 1945 the Attlee government had established the University Grants Committee and state funding came to represent an increasing proportion of the total. But, in 1963, the Robbins Report supported a national strategy for a massive expansion of higher education. Robbins is widely seen as a watershed in British higher education but, in reality, the report primarily validated a process already largely under way.

Established universities would be funded to take more students. Colleges of advanced technology, which had primarily been servicing the needs of local industry, would be accorded university status and a new wave of universities created. These new universities were built on greenfield campus sites. The University of Essex was near – but outside – Colchester, the University of Sussex near – but outside – Brighton. The University of Warwick was closer to the industrial city of Coventry than the bucolic town from which it took its name, but not within walking distance of either. The model was now one of residential campuses only loosely associated with the places where they were located. This detachment from community had major social, economic and industrial consequences.

In the 1960s the number of students taking degrees more than doubled and state expenditure on higher education rose by considerably more. The state's engagement with individual institutions through the University Grants Committee initially involved an extremely light touch. But this golden age of free-flowing cash and substantial autonomy did not last. Public expenditure came under pressure after 1975 and Margaret Thatcher was actively hostile to what she saw as increasingly left-wing institutions. A hotline to Whitehall would take the place of the address book of local grandees on the vice-chancellor's desk. In 1992 the centralization of tertiary education was completed, as polytechnics, which had been focussed on vocational training in their local communities, were converted to universities.

The centralizing instinct has been cross-party. The emasculation of local government became a Conservative agenda: the transfer of control over municipal finance to the Treasury was begun under Thatcher and continued under Osborne. Labour's instinct to centralize was still clearly alive and well in 2019. Its election manifesto proposed the creation of a National Education Service, a National Energy Agency, a National Care Agency, a National Food Commission, a National Youth Service, a National Investment Bank, a National Women's Commission and a National Refuge Fund.

MARKETS AND DECENTRALIZATION

A probably apocryphal story tells of the Soviet official who is sent on a mission to understand how capitalism functions in the United States. 'And who,' he asks, 'is in charge of the supply of bread to New York?' The answer, of course, is 'nobody'. Or perhaps 'everybody' – google 'supply of bread to New York' and you will obtain pages of listings. The supply of bread to New York is wholly decentralized and the result is a more reliable supply than Soviet central planners were able to achieve. Coordination is achieved not through central planning, but through decentralized competition within a market.

As we observed in Chapter 2, this ability of decentralized markets to achieve coordinated outcomes is perhaps the most important single insight of economics, and it is highly counter-intuitive. Surely central coordination is needed to secure reliability, and the elimination of duplication will increase efficiency? These propositions seemed, and seem, obvious – not just to ordinary people applying common sense, or to Soviet commissars planning mass industrialization, but to Western businesspeople. From John D. Rockefeller in the nineteenth century allegedly saying 'competition is a sin, we must destroy it', to Mike Coupe in 2018, the hapless chief executive of Sainsbury's, who was evidently unaware cameras were filming as he sang, 'We're in the money,' as he prepared to announce the merger of his business with Asda.*

But we live in a complex world which we only partially understand. Ministers, civil servants, regulators and high custodians of the public interest do not have and never can have the knowledge necessary to run a Central Electricity Authority or British Transport Commission, and the people who think they do are among the last people who should be in charge of them, or of anything else. It is because we have more than one supermarket chain that we learn how to run supermarkets, that shoppers discover what they want and do not want

* The incident probably did not encourage the Competition and Markets Authority to recognize the claimed merits of the deal; the CMA rejected the ludicrous assertion that the combined group would lower prices by 10 per cent and blocked the transaction.

from supermarkets, and managers come to interpret the needs of their customers. The relatively simple business of Walmart, the largest private sector employer in the world, taxes the capabilities of the best managers in the world. Even Walmart has only a quarter of the US retail grocery market and has struggled to find success outside the United States (which is why it had hoped to dispose of Asda to Sainsbury's). The somewhat less talented managers who can put up with the competing demands of politicians, doctors and patients naturally struggle with the far more complex business of running a national health-care monopoly.

If there were a single National Bread Service, everyone would recognize that its function – the provision of good-quality and affordable bread across the country – was vital; the purpose of the organization would become revered. But as we know from experience of planned economies, there would be recurrent bread shortages, as the executives in Bread House failed to anticipate the need for sandwiches for the school trip in Stornoway or the sudden rise in the popularity of focaccia in Faversham. What would be the most common explanation for persistent supply failures? That the service needed more money, a proposition that would seem to be confirmed when rapid increases in resources indeed improved the situation. The right answer, that bread should not be provided through a monopoly, and the best route to reliable bread supply is to decentralize decision-making to multiple suppliers in touch with local needs, is not the obvious one.

In Chapter 2 we reviewed and rejected the arguments of market fundamentalists – the claim that the freest possible markets are required in order to harness the ineradicable power of human greed for public benefit. The reason the market economy has been the only sustained route to prosperity around the world is not that rich countries are the most individualistic. If anything, the opposite is closer to the truth – rich countries are characterized by high levels of trust, cooperation and social cohesion. The reason market economies are successful is that they are intrinsically pluralist. They not only allow but encourage and facilitate experiment. But their pluralism is disciplined. If experiments fail – and most do – the market economy provides rapid feedback. Failures are abandoned, successes imitated. The repeated experience of centralized state control, in the West as in the Communist Bloc, was that there was reluctance to experiment, that experiments when made were on an inordinately large scale, and that acknowledgement and response to failure was a protracted process. There was an absence of either pluralism or discipline. From groundnuts through electricity generation to NHS computerization.

We need an effective state which does things that individuals and communities cannot do well, but which does not do things that the state cannot do well. At their best, our political parties immerse themselves in our aspirations and turn them into attainable common goals. But few of those goals are best achieved by national monopolies. The attachment to them is the fusion of two fallacies. One is the technocratic illusion of those who think they know the model: that top-down control is more efficient than devolved decision-taking. The other is that common purpose can be achieved only through the state: no other entities in the society are morally load-bearing – capable of forgoing selfishness for common purpose. The results have repeatedly fallen short of citizen expectations, undermining belief not only in the competence of governments but in their integrity. By 2019, according to the annual Edelman Survey, most people did not trust governments in either dimension.[8]

Trust in the state, and trust in politics, are inevitably intertwined. In the early post-war era they had succeeded together. By 2020, as the state had taken on functions for which less centralized organizations were better suited, and as the multiple pressures of individualism undermined common purpose, they were failing together. We have related the decline of trust in the state; we now turn to the decline of trust in political parties.

6

Shifting Political Tectonic Plates

'On the shoals of roast beef and apple pie, all socialist utopias
flounder.'

— Werner Sombart, *Why is There No Socialism*
in the United States?, 1906

By 2020 the erosion of trust in the traditional parties was an almost universal phenomenon around the societies of the West. And electoral upsets were a predictable result. But these upsets took a variety of different forms.

In the 2017 French presidential election, the candidates from the established left and right parties fell far behind the candidates of the extreme left and right, enabling the centrist Macron, whose En Marche movement was only a year old, to sail through the middle. Yet the very next year, he was facing his own mutiny from the Gilets Jaunes. In Germany in the same year the CDU and SPD together achieved barely 50 per cent of the vote; after some delay they formed a grand coalition which became increasingly precarious as support for both parties diminished. Both major German parties are already on their third subsequent leader, as the incumbents resigned in the face of electoral rejection.

In the United States in 2016 Trump, a populist with no political background or experience, was elected on a Republican ticket and united much, though by no means all, of that party's leadership and voting base behind his erratic pronouncements. In Italy a precarious government was formed in 2018 by what was described as the first all-populist government: a coalition of two parties of protest with little in the way of ideology or philosophy, which duly collapsed the following year into an equally precarious replacement.

The outcome of the Brexit referendum in 2016 upended the British political system. And in December 2019 Labour lost more than fifty seats to the Conservatives, almost all in working-class areas such as Stoke and Don Valley which had been traditional strongholds.

But these events were manifestations of much-longer-term trends. For a century, European politics had been defined ideologically by capitalism versus socialism, and voting behaviour largely determined by social class. The meanings of the terms 'capitalist' and 'socialist', and with them the left–right axis, had gradually lost definitional clarity. New terms – 'progressive', 'activist', 'populist' – had replaced them to describe political positions and groupings. Single-issue pressure groups, from Greenpeace to the Brexit Party, from Mermaids to Pegida, gained strength, while the membership of traditional parties diminished sharply.* And the historic link from social class to voting behaviour was completely severed.

The politics of the United States differs in that there has never been a socialist party or movement which has commanded significant support. That Bernie Sanders and Alexandria Ocasio-Cortez describe themselves as socialists is only a further demonstration of how far the political lexicon has shifted; theirs is not the socialism of Clement Attlee or François Hollande, far less Marx or Lenin. One of the authors recalls writing an essay in 1968 on the subject 'Why is European politics so much more ideological than that of the United States?' That was almost the last moment at which that essay topic could sensibly have been set. In 2020 the reverse appears to be the case, though it would be more accurate to call US politics tribal than ideological: Joe Biden is not an ideologue, nor Donald Trump.

---

* In most European countries, though not all, the voting strength of these traditional parties has also declined. Britain, whose voting system is particularly unfavourable to smaller parties, is a conspicuous exception.

THE RISE OF THE CENTRE

The terms 'left' and 'right' had entered politics in 1789, when opponents of the King sat to the left of the presiding officer in France's
Assemblée Nationale and royalists to the right. The use of the term to
describe political parties dates from France's Third Republic, whose
groupings designated themselves Centre Right, Centre Left, Extreme
Left and so on. As the franchise was extended, support for left-wing
parties grew and the left–right split polarized Europe in the 1930s and
led to its most destructive war.

In 1945 socialism was standing high in European working-class
esteem, although its support in the United States remained negligible.
While Roosevelt's bold pre-war policies had rescued US capitalism,
European governments had retreated into disastrous combinations of
nationalism and economic conservatism: after 1945 Europe's voters
wanted something different. Under communism, Russia had achieved
military victory over Germany, and most of Eastern Europe would
remain under Soviet domination until 1989. Russia tested a hydrogen
bomb in 1953 and launched a sputnik into space in 1957. Exaggerated
judgements of communist economic and technological achievements
remained widespread for another two decades.

Thus the inherited left–right axis continued to describe post-war
politics, though the spectrum of disagreement was far narrower
than in the interwar years. Britain's Labour government of 1945–51
brought into being a welfare state, much of which had been designed
during wartime by a Liberal. The Conservative government which
regained power in 1951 left that legacy more or less intact. There was
little practical difference between the stances of the major parties: by
the late 1950s the term 'Butskellism', named for the Conservative Rab
Butler and Labour's Hugh Gaitskell, was used to describe the wide-
ranging consensus.

In (West) Germany, the centre-right CDU led by Konrad Adenauer ruled in coalition with the liberal Free Democrats, before
entering a 'grand coalition' in 1966 with the centre-left SPD. In
the Iberian peninsula, the deaths of Franco and Salazar ended
Europe's twentieth-century engagement with far-right authoritarians.

Democratic politics was restored in these countries by moderate parties of left and right.

France's Fourth Republic (1946–58) was governed by unstable coalitions of moderates. The Algerian crisis, and the threat of a military coup, brought back to power General de Gaulle, the wartime leader of Free French forces. As peacetime leader, de Gaulle proved to be a figure keen on aggrandizement of his office and his country, but pragmatic in interpreting what that meant. Italian politics engaged many parties, with governments united only by their ineffectiveness and corruption.

MASS PROSPERITY

Such non-ideological politics enabled, and perhaps facilitated, an unprecedented transformation to mass prosperity. Germany recovered from the devastation of 1945 to become again a major economic power. In France, these years are still described as the 'Trente Glorieuses'. Britain enjoyed rapid growth and previously unimaginable low rates of unemployment, allegedly encapsulated in 1959 by the Conservative Prime Minister Harold Macmillan's slogan: 'You've never had it so good.'*

Werner Sombart, a German sociologist, had asked the question 'Why is there no socialism in the United States?' in his 1906 book and answered by observing the ability of the vast continent to feed its population well. Similarly, in post-war Europe, socialism foundered on the shoals of mass-produced cars, television and central heating. Most households acquired not only these goods but also washing machines, vacuum cleaners, refrigerators and telephones. In the wake of Labour's resounding defeat in the 1987 election, Ron Todd, Secretary-General of Britain's largest union, made the point with deadly accuracy: 'What do you say to a docker who earns £400 a week, owns his house, a new car, a microwave and a video, as well

---

* In fact, the reference comes from a speech at a Conservative rally in 1957 at which Macmillan, who had become premier six months earlier, told his supporters that 'many of our people have never had it so good'.

as a small place near Marbella? You do *not* say, "Let me take you out of your misery, brother."[1]

Households had more disposable income, which enabled them to afford these new consumer goods. Innovation in credit arrangements such as hire purchase – 'the never-never' – made these durables available even to others who did not, and the surge in demand allowed economies of scale which greatly reduced prices. This followed a century which had given most households indoor toilets and running water, electric light and enough housing space to make it possible for adult couples to enjoy their own room. A century in which public health and medical advances had cured many infectious diseases and drastically reduced infant mortality. The lives of women, in particular, were transformed as desired family sizes required fewer pregnancies and the burden of domestic work was reduced. Ironically, the availability of television sets in Eastern Europe enabled its citizens to see how much more effective market economies had been than socialist direction in bringing many of these changes into the lives of ordinary people.

Inequality was reducing in ways which did not really show up in aggregate statistics and Gini coefficients. The rich had never had to fetch water, stoke fires or scrub clothes on a washboard. They could travel more than a few miles from home – even visit foreign countries. Now these things were true for almost everyone in developed societies. Many middle-class households had employed servants. Now they could no longer afford them, but technology meant that they did not need them.

THE DECLINE OF THE CENTRE

Just as the Second World War had bequeathed a confident state, it had bequeathed a confident left. In the United States the left was defined by the policies of the New Deal; in Europe by socialism. And in Britain, as we have seen, left-wing politics also meant the centralized state. The parties of the right had no big ideas of their own and slowly acquiesced in many of these policies.

Perhaps the transition away from this political centrism began in the 1960s in America. Johnson's embrace of the civil rights of African Americans after Kennedy's assassination in 1963 ruptured the coalition of northern liberals and conservative southerners which had supported Roosevelt and Kennedy. Far from being an early manifestation of individualism, the policy was a shamefully belated acceptance of African Americans into the national community. But, soon after, the war in Vietnam polarized the nation by age and education, triggering the student protests of 1968 and creating an organized left detached from the working class, whose own children were being conscripted into the military. The generation of '68, still known in France as the *soixante-huitards*, was the antecedent to the young-middle-class activism which almost fifty years later filled Zuccotti Park and St Paul's churchyard, helped elect Obama twice and enabled Sanders to derail two Democratic primary campaigns. As we have described, wartime expenditure immediately followed by the oil shock of the early 1970s further contributed to inflation and ended the sustained economic growth which had drawn much of the heat from political argument. People lost confidence in their governments, and governments lost confidence in their ability to manage.

The half-century after the 1929 Wall Street Crash and the depression which followed had left a finance sector cowed and closely regulated. But from the 1960s finance came to exert a greater influence on the real economy and on the government. Financialization had multiple causes – new technologies in data processing and transmission not only made possible transactions of previously unimagined complexity but, like faster air travel, made the world appear a smaller place. In Britain, a meritocratic culture in finance replaced an old-boy network of people who trusted each other because they had been to the same school, a change accelerated by the arrival of foreigners who did not realize the significance of the 'raising of the eyebrows' of the Governor of the Bank of England.

The outcome was a combination of deregulation and reregulation. Those who blame the financial crisis on deregulation fail to recognize that there is today, and was in 2008, far more financial regulation than ever before: the state was increasingly active, yet decreasingly effective. The spectacular rise of the financial sector in the UK and the US created a powerful new lobby, and some equally spectacular incomes. Both the scale of activity and the scale of reward needed justification, and such justification was found in a combination of market fundamentalism and expressive individualism. The level of profitability of the activity was itself deemed demonstrative of its value to society, and the extraordinary level of remuneration indicative of the special talents of those who received it: 'I earned my bonus. I deserve it.'

Robert Gordon has, controversially, argued that there was a critical change after 1970 in the evolution of technology.[2] The preceding century had been without precedent in the impact of innovation on everyday life. Innovation in consumer goods certainly continued after 1970, but mostly it was incremental rather than transformational. The difference between an automatic washing machine with forty-three programmes and the twin tubs our mothers were thrilled to buy is small relative to the difference between the twin tub and the washboard. A large-screen television with an OLED display is better than the small black-and-white set around which neighbours gathered to watch the 1953 Coronation, or the larger and more reliable ones on which families saw England's 1966 World Cup victory, but the big change had been the ability to watch the Coronation, or major sporting events, *as they happened*, at all. The most important modern consumer innovations are perhaps the mobile phone, the personal computer, the internet and low-cost air travel, all of them most important to the young and well educated. The washing machine and the vacuum cleaner had been transformative primarily for the working-class housewife. If the inventions of the years from 1950 to 1970 had changed life most for her, those of 1990 to 2010 changed them most for middle-class singles.

Poorer macroeconomic performance; the greater role of finance in economic policies; the slower pace of consumer-goods innovation: there are many reasons why a political consensus around the comfortable centrism of the 1950s and 1960s eroded. We will describe further causes below. But, whatever the origins, the outcome is clear. And, as consensus eroded, different variants of the new elite individualism infiltrated the established parties of both left and right, displacing pragmatism and driving them in different directions.

THE DECLINE OF THE
CONFIDENT LEFT

We may never know the extent to which 1960s fears of communist economic success were the product of conspicuous, but fundamentally unimportant, Russian technological achievement (the sputnik), of faulty intelligence or of scaremongering based on willful misinterpretation of that intelligence.

But, beginning with the suppression of the Hungarian Revolution of 1956, and the Prague Spring of 1968, communism discredited itself in the countries whose regimes professed it. By the time of the opening of the Berlin Wall in 1989 and the final collapse of the Soviet Union which followed, the evidence of communist economic failure was unambiguous. The division of Germany into two zones was perhaps the greatest controlled experiment in economic history – and the results were decisive. Productivity and real incomes in the socialist East were only a fraction of those achieved in the market economy of the West.

European working-class support for communism had dwindled steadily since the Second World War. In Britain, socialist ideology enjoyed a brief resurgence in 1974 when the defeat of the government in two miners' strikes gave trade unions a glimpse of power. But in 1976 Britain's Labour government was forced to seek a humiliating loan from the International Monetary Fund, and newly appointed Prime Minister James Callaghan told the Labour Party Conference, 'We used to think that you could spend your way out of a recession, and increase employment by cutting taxes and boosting government spending. I tell you in all candour that that option no longer exists.'[3] By 1981, when François Mitterand was elected President of France with a socialist programme, fiscal and economic realities forced a rapid reversal. For at least two generations, socialism in Western democracies was at an end, and the mainstream European left simply abandoned it. Even the initial post-war successes of social democracy had eroded. In Sweden, the beacon of European social democracy, the Social Democratic Party, which had governed without interruption since 1932, was defeated in 1976.

Socialist and Marxist factions remained, within and outside the major parties, but had been reduced to an extremist rump. As with other ideologues, the members of that rump were not interested in delivering practical policies: to an increasing extent, their remaining activists were fanatics whose priority was protest and whose principal enemies were often those who espoused slightly different versions of their own beliefs. Through the 1970s, strident British Marxists such as Derek Hatton and Arthur Scargill rose to prominence, while Militant Tendency, a Trotskyite grouping, successfully organized infiltration of the Labour Party. Since this ideological extremism had no resonance with most voters, it drove Labour into the electoral catastrophe of 1983.

The traditional ideologies of the left had faded, but the traditional parties of the left survived them – for a time. In both Britain and the United States, these parties were fortunate to have found clever and charismatic leaders in Tony Blair and Bill Clinton. Under amorphous brands – 'New Labour', 'the Third Way', 'triangulation' – they repositioned their parties to a pragmatic mixture of the priorities of the decreasingly influential working class and those of the rising class of educated youth who favoured global salvationism and the individualism of the new meritocracy. Blair promised to be 'tough on crime' and Clinton supported 'three strikes and you're out', but Blair's Chancellor of the Exchequer raised benefits and Clinton's wife tried to reform health insurance. Meritocracy demanded that the brightest should rise regardless of initial circumstances, hence the new focus on access to education and improving its quality through Academy or Charter schools, to which Blair added a national programme for pre-school education. Their combination of policies that appealed to both constituencies and personal magnetism was enough to hold their parties' diverging support together. Obama performed the same magic, but Blair had no equivalent successor. Labour's electoral disaster of 1983 would be repeated in 2019, when a combination of the emoting youth who had chanted, 'Oh, Jeremy Corbyn,' at Glastonbury and the extremists of Momentum who had infiltrated the party delivered a comfortable victory to Boris Johnson.

THE PROBLEMS OF THE RIGHT

The immediate consequence of socialist decline was electoral success for the right. In Sweden, a rightist coalition came to power in 1976. In Britain, Margaret Thatcher became Prime Minister in May 1979. And in the United States' 1980 election, Ronald Reagan ousted Jimmy Carter.

But the changing political environment posed problems for the parties of the right as well as those of the left. In Europe, the left had identified itself for a century with socialism, and this identification had defined the political spectrum not just for those who favoured socialism but also for those who opposed or felt threatened by it. These rightist parties included economic liberals who believed in the virtues of untrammelled free markets; businesspeople who rarely mustered the same enthusiasm for competition but sought freedom from government regulation; financiers in search of more opportunities to enrich themselves; social conservatives who believed in the virtues of Church and tradition; militaristic nationalists, aristocrats and other well-bred persons threatened by social mobility; and the nouveaux riches who were the beneficiaries of that social mobility but shared the desire of those with inherited wealth to secure lower taxes. People who had little in common except that they opposed socialism. And when socialism ceased to be a pressing threat they discovered they had little else in common.

The failure of Labour to provide effective opposition in the 1980s, aided by the foolish hubris of an Argentinian dictator, left Thatcher free to pursue her own agenda, and she found much of it in the tenets of market fundamentalism, with its accompanying embrace of possessive individualism and dismissal of 'society'. In the course of a decade, she and the ideologies she promoted shifted permanently the location of the centre ground of politics, not just in Britain but around the world. But her own foolish hubris was eventually too much for her party, and in 1990 she was deposed in favour of the thoroughly non-ideological John Major. Ronald Reagan's presidency ended in 1989 and he was similarly succeeded by the more pragmatic George H. W. Bush.

The right seemed to be returning pragmatically to the centre. But by the 1990s globalization and technology were changing patterns of production in ways which had major social and economic consequences, with manufacturing jobs outsourced to Asia or replaced by robots. A responsive pragmatism would have addressed the new anxieties which resulted from these changes. But the shrivelling of the membership of the political parties had gradually changed their composition, detaching them from the people who were being adversely affected. As Ken Clarke, one of the many pragmatists of the time who enjoyed much greater affection from the electorate than from their own party, recently admitted:

> The mistake we, the Establishment, made internationally was in the 1990s and 2000s when it was all going well – when we thought we'd really sorted out a marvellous new world . . . We didn't, I think, know quite what to do about the at least 50 per cent of the population for whom this meant their living standards didn't rise, jobs they'd be proud of were given up for ones that are a way of earning a living, paying the bills . . . In practical, day-to-day terms, *we've made a bit of a cock-up of it* [authors' emphasis].[4]

Retiring from politics in 2019, Clarke had seen the electoral victory of his party but had also seen that party become one which no longer reflected his values. And intellectual Republicans had experienced the same combination of electoral success with moral and intellectual failure.

The 'cock-ups' of the centre which Clarke described had led to its implosion. The state, over which the centre had presided, had systematically and persistently assumed tasks which had been beyond its capacity to perform. And the state and business together had proved inadequate not only at providing fulfilling jobs which sustained the dignity of the half that did not go to university – as Clarke had noted – but also failed to meet the risen expectations of those of their children who, newly debt-ridden, had joined the ranks of the half which now did. And where, amid all this failure, was the party of the left, the Labour Party that in 1945 had been swept into power by a working class that trusted it to address their concerns?

7

How Labour Lost the
Working Class

'I love the poorly educated.'
    – Donald Trump, victory speech after the
    Nevada Primary, 23 February 2016

In 1945 the British working class overwhelmingly placed its trust in the Labour Party, giving it a huge majority in parliament. The party's programme for government, drafted by Michael Young, had addressed practical working-class anxieties: notably, health, education and unemployment. By 2019, that trust had evaporated. The most remarkable feature of Britain's 2019 general election was the loss by Labour of seats in which the party's vote had once been weighed rather than counted. Trust had still been there in 1966, when Labour secured 75 per cent of the votes in Don Valley and 72 per cent in Stoke-on-Trent North. Yet in 2019 the Conservative Party won both constituencies with comfortable majorities.

While the Labour Party had provided the impetus for policies that helped the working class, for thirty years post-1945 the Conservative Party had been sufficiently pragmatic to absorb those changes that appeared to work well. This chapter tells the story of the unravelling of this pro-working-class consensus as both parties became infected with individualist ideas, as the centralized state became overloaded (Chapter 5), and as the established party structures disintegrated (Chapter 6). We begin our story by returning to Don Valley and Stoke.

THE MARGINALIZATION OF THE
BRITISH WORKING CLASS

Don Valley is on the former South Yorkshire coalfield and incor-
porates part of the city of Doncaster and some of the surrounding
countryside. Stoke-on-Trent is famous for its potteries; the city com-
prises the 'six towns' celebrated by Arnold Bennett. Today you will
still find the head offices of Wedgwood and other ceramic businesses
in Stoke, but much of the production has been outsourced to Asia.
The low-skilled jobs in Doncaster – today a major logistics and ware-
housing centre – lack the pride and solidarity men found in vanished
mining. Where once Stoke made world-famous ceramics, now the main
enterprise there is Bet365: working to fleece low-income gamblers
may offer less job satisfaction. Both constituencies are economically
depressed, although by no means the most deprived in the country:
among the UK's 650 constituencies, they are ranked respectively 434
and 582.[1]* In the most deprived English seat of all – Liverpool Walton
– Labour won 85 per cent of the vote in 2019.

The decline of the Labour Party in areas such as Doncaster and
Stoke has been long, slow and relentless. In 1966 Labour's margin
of votes over the Conservatives was 6 per cent nationally, but 50 per
cent in Don Valley and 43 per cent in Stoke North – implying a local
out-performance relative to the national picture of 44 per cent in Don
Valley and 37 per cent in Stoke.[2] Table 1 overleaf illustrates the steady
reduction in Labour's local advantage in the elections that followed.

Labour's decline in many of its traditional strongholds is not simply
attributable to Corbyn's inadequacies as leader and recent concern
over Brexit; these issues only accelerated and crystallized trends which
had been in progress for fifty years. Leave won 72 per cent of the vote
in Stoke North and 68 per cent in Don Valley, but this was a *reflection*
rather than the *cause* of underlying long-term disaffection from not
only national but traditional local politics.[3] In both Doncaster and

* For Stoke-on-Trent we use the data from the constituency of Stoke-on-Trent
North; the data from Stoke-on-Trent South and Stoke-on-Trent Central tell a similar
story.

Local Labour majority over Conservatives relative to the national majority, %, average

	Don Valley	Stoke North
Before Thatcher (1966, 1970, 1974 x2)	42	34
Thatcher years (1979, 1983, 1987, 1992)	28	29
Blair years (1997, 2001, 2005)	22	34
Post-Blair (2010, 2015, 2017)	17	16
2019	−10	−16

Source: House of Commons Library (17 Apr. 2020).

Stoke, maverick independents had won election as mayor long before Brexit became a significant political issue.

Don Valley and Stoke North are representative of the smaller industrial towns outside the south-east, the areas in which Labour's traditional support finally collapsed in 2019. Peter Hain was member of parliament for Neath, a former mining constituency in South Wales, from 1991 to 2015. In 1966, Labour won 80 per cent of the votes in Neath. In Hain's first general election candidacy, in 1992, Labour's share was still 68 per cent. He last fought the seat in 2010, winning with 46 per cent of the vote. In 2019, the successful Labour candidate obtained barely half of the party's share fifty-three years earlier – only 43 per cent. On the day following the election, Hain commented:

> I've noticed how the whole base of the Labour Party has dissolved under our feet, as it were, in old strongholds like Neath and right across the South Wales valleys. Those organic links between big trade unions in mines and heavy industry and so on, and then social clubs, welfare clubs, rugby clubs and so on, that organic link between the party and those community roots has basically just dissolved.[4]

In emphasizing the decline of community in traditional working-class areas, Hain had identified Labour's central problem. His assessment pointed to much broader issues in changing structures of political allegiance – and also hinted at keys to solutions.

And, in a paradoxical way, Liverpool Walton, which has moved politically in the opposite direction, also illustrates the relationship between community structure and political allegiance. Liverpool Walton, now the safest Labour seat in the country, elected a Conservative member of parliament throughout the 1950s. For much of the twentieth century, the heavily working-class cities of Liverpool and Glasgow were far more Conservative than their social composition would have suggested. This was the result of the sectarian division between the Irish Catholic community and the assertive Protestant majority, which mapped into Labour and Conservative political affiliation. Only when the influence of the churches and the militant Protestant Orange Order declined were religious divisions reduced to the milder disagreement between rival supporters of Everton and Liverpool football clubs, ceasing to have much political significance.*

As the 1950s anomalies of Conservative strength in Liverpool and Glasgow were resolved, by 1967 the political scientist Peter Pulzer could write: 'Class is the basis of British party politics; all else is embellishment and detail.'⁵ By 2019, such a claim would be ridiculous: the class basis of political identification had entirely dissolved. Indeed, to the extent that it mattered, it had reversed. The Conservatives had stronger appeal to C2DE voters (broadly working class) than to ABC1 voters (broadly middle class), their lead over Labour being fifteen points among the former and only ten points among the latter.⁶

In consequence, Labour had become a seemingly impossible alliance. Liverpool Walton – the most deprived seat in the country – which Labour had only narrowly won in 1964 – had reverted to class type

* Which is not to say that Liverpool politics became normal; the breakdown of its traditional structures created a vacuum. For a time, the Liberals (as they then were) controlled the city. In 1981 race riots in Toxteth raged for nine days and CS gas was used to disperse crowds; in direct consequence, Conservative minister Michael Heseltine was appointed to spearhead a remarkably successful urban-regeneration programme; at around the same time the Trotskyite Militant group gained control of the local Labour Party and managed the city council with comprehensive irresponsibility until its leader, Derek Hatton, was expelled from the party and tried, though acquitted, on corruption charges.

and become that party's safest seat. But Kensington – the constituency with the highest per capita income in Britain – was Labour's most astonishing gain in 2017 (the party only narrowly failed to retain it in 2019). Similarly, Edinburgh South, Scotland's most affluent constituency, is now Labour's only Scottish seat. Labour's campaign priorities built an alliance between the minority of people so poor that their primary interest was in higher benefits and the minority of people so rich that their primary interest was expressive: the superior intensity of their feelings of empathy.

THE END OF CLASS-BASED ALLEGIANCE

To understand voting behaviour in Britain today, we need to look at the influence of age and education, without which we cannot understand Kensington, and the role of communities, without which we cannot understand Liverpool Walton and Neath, Don Valley and Stoke North. These factors are, of course, interrelated.

If class no longer determines voting behaviour, the impact of age is clear. Among those between the ages of eighteen and twenty-four, Labour leads by thirty-five percentage points; for those over seventy, the Conservative margin is fifty-three points.[7] The gradient is a steady one: thirty-nine is the age at which a voter is equally likely to support either party. Is this a cohort effect – are those born around the turn of the century natural Labour supporters while those born in 1950 are natural Conservatives? Since those born in 1950 became the revolutionary *soixante-huitards* of 1968 before voting Conservative in retirement, the latter explanation seems unlikely. Perhaps, as Benjamin Disraeli is reputed to have observed: 'A man who is not a Liberal at sixteen has no heart; a man who is not a Conservative at sixty has no head.'*

---

* There does not seem to be any reliable evidence that he actually *did* say this. There is some controversy about where the idea comes from; the earliest form we have found is a conversation between John Adams and a Dr Ewen in which Adams said, 'A boy of fifteen who is not a democrat is good for nothing, and he is no better who is a democrat at twenty.' (T. Jefferson (1799)).

But the effects of age and education are inseparable. The Conservative lead among those with only GCSE qualifications or less was thirty-three points; the Labour lead among those with degrees was 14 per cent.[8] But only 8 per cent of those born in 1950 went to university, compared with about half the population today, so graduates as a group are much younger than the population as a whole.[9]

The decline of class-based voting has been associated with a steady fall in partisan alignment. In 1966, only 12 per cent of voters chose a party other than the one they had supported at the previous election in 1964; in 2015, 43 per cent of voters had changed allegiance since 2010, and third parties gained their highest-ever aggregate share of the vote in a British election. In 2017, disloyalty was still high but the two main parties had resumed dominance.[10] British politics is far more fluid than in the past. This provides new opportunities for pragmatists – but also for populists and demagogues.

The shift from social class to age and education as determinants of voting behaviour is not a specifically British phenomenon resulting from differences of view over the country's appropriate relationship with the European Union. Nor is it recent. A similar change is common to most Western democracies and has been evolving over several decades. In the US in 2016, Clinton defeated Trump by eighteen points among those aged between eighteen and twenty-nine but was 8 per cent behind with voters over sixty-five. Trump outperformed Clinton among those with no college education, but Clinton was easily ahead with graduates. Most strikingly of all, white men without college education voted for Trump by sixty-seven to twenty-eight per cent.[11]

Indeed, the reversal of the relationship between occupationally defined social class and voting behaviour is even more marked in the US than in the UK. As Richard Florida writes, 'What we are witnessing is nothing less than a great inversion of America's political geography. Dating back to the 1930s, the blue-collar working class once provided the backbone of the Democratic electorate, but today, states with larger working-class populations have swung solidly into the Republican camp. And blue (Democrat) states have become those where the knowledge, professional, and service workers that make up the creative class predominate.'[12] To find a Clinton voter, look among manicurists in California or doctors in New York; to locate a Trump supporter, find a welder in Wyoming or a truck driver in Alabama.

THE RISE OF THE MERITOCRACY

Michael Young's 1958 book *The Rise of the Meritocracy*, which gave the English language a new word, was – it is now sometimes forgotten – a satire. Ostensibly written in 2033, it depicted a society in which social position was the result of talent rather than birth: and this was presented *as a dystopia*. Almost fifty years after drafting Labour's 1945 manifesto, Young – by then Lord Young – observed that much of what he feared had come to pass. 'It is hard indeed,' he wrote in words that may be needed for Labour's tombstone, 'in a society that makes so much of merit, to be judged as having none. *No underclass has ever been left as morally naked as that* [authors' emphasis].'[13]

Labour had come into being as the party of the underclass. While Denis Healey, Labour Chancellor of the Exchequer from 1974 to 1980, never actually said he would squeeze the rich till the pips squeak, a generation of political commentators believed he had, and he did raise income tax rates to a maximum of 83 per cent. Neil Kinnock, the last Labour leader to have come from a working-class background – although Kinnock himself had attended university, his father had been a miner – was also the last to reject the harsh implications of meritocracy. 'I warn you not to be ordinary,' he said in a famous speech attacking Thatcherite priorities in the 1983 election campaign, 'I warn you not to be young, I warn you not to fall sick, I warn you not to grow old.'[14] But not enough of the ordinary, the young, the sick and the old rallied to Kinnock's call and Labour suffered its most crushing defeat.

As the composition of the Labour Party changed, working-class priorities gave way successively to the ideologies of individualism. By the time that Labour swept back to power in 1997, the party had unambiguously embraced meritocracy. Blair and Brown had committed not to reverse the income tax cut from 83 per cent to 40 per cent introduced by the Conservatives. If some people became 'filthy rich', in the words of Peter Mandelson, New Labour was 'intensely relaxed' about it.[15]

The ordinary, the young, the ill and the old of Kinnock's concern would be compensated with higher benefits. As long as the economy roared ahead and the filthy rich paid their taxes (an often-ignored caveat which Mandelson had expressed), these benefits could be financed.

Oxford-educated Blair, son of a barrister, and Mandelson, grandson of Herbert Morrison, embraced meritocracy. Brown (son of the manse and student rector of Edinburgh University) personified the leader who thinks he 'knows the model': accepting many of the premises of market fundamentalism but believing in the capacity of the tax and benefit system to deal with undesirable consequences.* Brown vigorously deployed monitored incentives throughout the public sector in the pursuit of global salvationism.

THE PRETENSIONS OF THE MERITOCRACY

But this new Labour realignment missed the point which Young had understood when he wrote of the 'morally naked' underclass – that people need to feel valued by the society in which they live. As opportunities for skilled manual work diminished, especially in provincial Britain, which was distant from the spending of the 'filthy rich', what the underclass wanted was not higher benefits but new opportunities. Benefits-financed consumption was not a substitute for the dignity of earning a decent living.

In *The Intellectuals and the Masses*, published in 1992, John Carey observed the widening gap between the meritocracy and the actual lives of the working classes whose cause many of them affected to espouse. 'Arnold Bennett is the hero of this book,' he wrote of the chronicler of Stoke and its region.[16] Virginia Woolf – the quintessentially self-conscious intellectual – cited Bennett mockingly for his interest in the mundane materialist concerns of the society he described. 'Most of the dwellings were owned by their occupiers, who, each an absolute monarch of the soil, niggled in his sooty garden of

* Thus accepting the validity of the Second Theorem of Welfare Economics as well as the First.

an evening amid the flutter of drying shirts and towels. Freehold Villas symbolised the final triumph of Victorian economics, the apotheosis of the prudent and industrious artisan. It corresponded with a Building Society Secretary's dream of paradise.' 'One line of insight,' Woolf wrote contemptuously 'would have done more than all these lines of description.'[17]

But her self-awarded 'insight' did not extend beyond Bloomsbury, whereas Freehold Villas did indeed represent the aspirations of many of the inhabitants of the towns. The people for whom the difference between freehold and feudal copyhold – Woolf laughs at Bennett's attention to this point – was of real importance. Many of them were later enabled to buy their freehold villas with the aid of Thatcher's 'right to buy' scheme and the Building Society.

New Labour had failed to recognize this because it had become too detached from the values of ordinary people. The party was now dominated by public sector professionals such as teachers. Unsurprisingly, many of them had taken business at its word: if it was indeed driven only to 'maximize shareholder value', they asked the inevitable question we posed in Chapter 2: 'Why should we let them do that?' They took pride in their own scruples in avoiding private sector employment, perhaps gilded by resentment at having forgone the chance of the higher earnings that were so publicly displayed by the greedy. The claim to moral superiority became manifest in an obsessive concern that the NHS should not be contaminated by any interface with business.

A sense of moral superiority came to suffuse the left. An activist group was capturing the party for a radically different agenda in which the provincial working class were seen as at best peripheral. In 2015 it turned on New Labour as morally compromised by a grubby concern with winning elections. The Democrats had experienced a similar takeover: Hillary Clinton's reference to the 'deplorables' did indeed reveal the true colours of the progressive meritocracy. Corbyn personified expressive individualism, attracting a fan club admiring the intensity of the passion he brought to protest as performance, initially forgiving of his manifest lack of knowledge.

As membership of the Conservative Party shrivelled, a small group of enthusiasts for market fundamentalism, libertarianism and possessive individualism had wielded considerable influence between 1979 and 2010. But when working-class voters drifted away from Labour, the electoral advantages of pragmatism fitfully crept back in: Cameron, May and Johnson, each non-ideological in very different ways, successively increased the Conservative working-class vote.

In 2017 Theresa May, with extraordinary political ineptitude, rapidly dissipated a massive lead in the opinion polls by proposing to confiscate Freehold Villas should its owner succumb to Alzheimer's disease: many of her potential supporters warily reverted to Labour. But by 2019 the Conservatives had learned from their mistake. Stoke would strike back at the contempt of Woolf and her ilk.

SOMEWHERES AND ANYWHERES

In his 2001 appraisal Young wrote that, with the coming of the meritocracy, 'the now leaderless masses were partially disfranchised; as time has gone by, more and more of them have been disengaged, and disaffected to the extent of not even bothering to vote'. Young noted that the two dominant figures setting the policy of the 1945 Labour government were Ernest Bevin and Herbert Morrison, both of whom had left school at eleven. He went on to observe that 'They [the working class] no longer have their own people to represent them. They have been deprived by educational selection of many of those who would have been their natural leaders, the able spokesmen and spokeswomen from the working class who continued to identify with the class from which they came.' Young anticipated what happened in Don Valley and Stoke, where the defeated Labour candidates both had degrees, and were both from the south.*

* To her credit, Caroline Flint, the former MP for Don Valley, was living in the constituency and had become all too aware of the gulf between her constituents and Corbyn's Labour Party, which duly denounced her. At the time of writing, Ms Flint is threatened with legal action by Emily Thornberry, MP for Islington South (Labour majority 17,228), for alleging that Ms Thornberry told Ms Flint that she (Ms Thornberry) was fortunate that her constituents were not as stupid as Ms Flint's. The vignette tells much about Labour's future prospects in seats such as Don Valley. Ruth Smeeth, defeated in Stoke North, went to school near Stoke but left to go to university and did not return until adopted as candidate for what was then still a safe Labour seat.

In this new meritocracy, membership of the elite is determined by education rather than class. A future Ernest Bevin and Herbert Morrison would almost certainly have been among the half of the population going to university. Not only did this selection out of the working class make the political class less representative – and less responsive to real working-class needs – but it removed similarly talented young people from their communities. The cumulative effect of this removal of educated young people from Don Valley and Stoke is revealed in the latest census (2011). Don Valley has one of the lowest student populations of any constituency. Stoke North is around average, not because children brought up in Stoke stay there to attend university, but because it offers inexpensive accommodation to students spending three years at Keele.

David Goodhart focussed on this issue in distinguishing between anywheres and somewheres. Many readers of his book *The Road to Somewhere* will be surprised to learn that *most people in Britain still live within twenty miles of the place they lived in when they were fourteen*.[18] Like the authors, and Ms Flint and Ms Smeeth (MP for Stoke-on-Trent North from 2015 to 2019), many of those readers left their home towns to go to university or to find work and have never lived there since, but return as privileged visitors; like the authors, they have frequent-flyer cards and converse comfortably with members of a similar elite in capital cities around the world. They have become anywheres. And they are slow to understand the sense of place, neighbourhood and community which still matter to somewheres – who comprise most of the electorate in Don Valley, Neath and Stoke.

And few issues are more likely to produce different responses from anywheres and somewheres than immigration and Brexit. This difference continues to bewilder many anywheres. Perhaps the anywheres should get out more, on buses rather than aeroplanes. If they did, they might more easily understand the salience of these issues in the past decade.

And anywheres tend to raise anywheres, and somewheres somewheres. Cultures are transmitted through families, and in the world of meritocracy, the – considerable – extent to which disparities are still transmitted down generations is reinforced through the catchment areas of the educational system. Parents who have themselves been successful are able to create better opportunities for their children by equipping them to navigate the new meritocracy, rather than educating them in appropriate manners and accents. And, unlike the somewheres, they can finance their children to take 'gap years'. In Switzerland and all the Nordic countries, there are forms of conscription, often run by lottery and offering non-military but socially purposive options, in which middle-class youths waiting for university may spend time alongside their working-class peers.* But in Britain, and most other rich countries, the gap year is typically devoted to some morally impressive activity, or just exotic travel, appealingly located somewhere spatially remote, but not as culturally remote as working with the underclass.

Unsurprisingly, the working-class resentment which had once been directed at aristocrats and capitalists is now directed at the metropolitan elite of anywheres – politicians, journalists, academics, lawyers and bankers. The problem was aggravated when the 2008 financial crisis revealed that many members of this modern elite were not even very good at the activities which yielded them privileged positions and high incomes.

Of course, Boris Johnson (Eton and Oxford) and Donald Trump (New York real-estate developer, like his father, and a graduate of Wharton, one of the world's top-ranked business schools) are themselves supreme products of privilege, and so, superficially, it seems puzzling that working-class voters favour them. But as Amy Chua observes, Trump 'in terms of tastes, sensibilities and values, actually *is* similar to the white working class . . . with the way he talks (locker room), dresses, shoots from the hip, gets caught making mistakes'.[19] Johnson's irreverent humour and chaotic personal lifestyle have given him an even more potent anti-establishment appeal, effective with both metropolitan youth, who helped elect him Mayor of London, and provincial working-class voters, who helped make him Prime Minister. And Johnson gave the impression of being a pragmatist, attuned to working-class concerns. He ditched the lingering residue of market fundamentalism reflected in the tax-cutting and

---

* Nor are these seen as anachronisms. Sweden abolished conscription in 2010 but decided to reintroduce it in 2017.

fiscal parsimony priorities of Osborne and Hammond, and switched from maximizing the growth of GDP to talk of levelling-up provincial Britain and controlling immigration. Refuting Thatcher's famous phrase, he declared 'there really *is* such a thing as society'. Where once the provincial working class trusted Labour's Clement Attlee, now it has placed its trust, or at least its support, in the hands of the Conservatives' Boris Johnson. How can he, or any other leader of a modern society, best deliver on it?

PART III
Community

8

Our Communitarian Nature

'Man is by nature a social animal; an individual who is unso-
cial naturally and not accidentally is either beneath our notice
or more than human. Society is something that precedes the
individual. Anyone who either cannot lead the common life
or is so self-sufficient as not to need to, and therefore does not
partake of society, is either a beast or a god.'

– Aristotle, *Politics, c.*330BC

'The ideas of economists and political philosophers, both when they are right and when they are wrong, are more powerful than is commonly understood. Indeed, the world is ruled by little else. Practical men, who believe themselves to be quite exempt from any intellectual influences, are usually slaves of some defunct economist.' Keynes's words are no less true today than in 1936. Having described the damage done by ideas that shrunk society to a struggle between individuals and the state, we turn to the philosophy and the science that introduce the actor missing from that shrivelled view – community.

Philosophers such as Rawls and Nozick, superficially contrasting, both claimed to achieve justice by treating the selfish individual as axiomatic but withdrawing that individual from any particular society. The language of rights claims universalism – the rights it identifies are rights in all places and for all times. If some societies fail to value or fulfil these rights, that is the product of *their* pre-enlightenment state of ignorance.

The communitarian approach we advocate in this chapter and those that follow makes two central, related claims. We believe that humans are not selfish, maximizing individuals, pursuing their own conception of happiness: they seek fulfilment which arises largely from their inter-action with others – in families, in streets and villages, at work and in many other forms of association. And we claim that agency – moral, social and economic – is not polarized between the individual and the state, but that society is made up of a rich, interacting web of group activities through which individuals find that fulfilment. We return to the notion of civil society – a term which is now often used to refer only to the activities of NGOs but which we will use in its historic, much more general sense.

Both these ideas – of human flourishing and of civil society – are first articulated, as is so much, by Aristotle. Human purpose is *eudai-monia*, the life well lived, and the measure of a good society is its ability to create conditions conducive to flourishing. This is a very different measure from that given by the aggregate of the utilities of rational maximizing selfish individuals. Fulfilment is the product of the realization of virtues – honesty, courage, compassion, patience, fair dealing.

But to flourish requires balance and moderation, even in virtues. Honesty does not require us to tell our children the truth about their artistic or sporting prowess. Too little patience is a vice, but so is too much. Compassion is admirable, but the virtue of compassion is the practical compassion that helps the neighbour in distress rather than the global salvationism of Mrs Jellyby. There are no absolutes – as there were for Kant, who insisted that the obligation to tell the truth required us to inform a would-be murderer of the whereabouts of his victim, or as there are for the modern human rights lawyer who ensures that a convicted drug gang cannot be deported.

So is the communitarian route to fulfilment any more likely to deliver it than the false promises of individualism? Adam Smith char-acterizes *eudaimonia* as 'deserving of love'. Economic Man, greedy, selfish, lazy unless properly incentivized, is not deserving of love, and little in modern psychology suggests he is capable of fulfilment. The psychologist Abraham Maslow's hierarchy of needs prioritizes the economic necessities of survival, but once these are achieved, he claims, we seek belonging, esteem and, finally, self-actualization.[1] Self-actualization, it should be emphasized, is not posting a selfie to

Instagram or some other manifestation of expressive identity; self-actualization, which Maslow suggested only a tiny minority were able to achieve, means realizing one's full potential, being the best that one can be. Martin Seligman has pioneered the psychology of well-being. But for its lack of elegance, his conclusion – 'while relationships are not everything, they are almost everything' – might echo Smith or Aristotle. Freedom of agency is only meaningful in the context of relationships.[2]

COMMUNITY

Communities are most immediately associated with place. But there are many other kinds of community – religious denominations, sports clubs and book clubs, bird-watchers and alumni groups, the varieties of cooperative activity whose decline Robert Putnam would lament in *Bowling Alone*.

Civil society is comprised of associations which share values and norms. In 1767, the Scottish Enlightenment philosopher Adam Ferguson – contemporary and sometimes friend of Adam Smith – composed an 'An Essay on the History of Civil Society'. As a young man, Ferguson had been chaplain to the Black Watch, a regiment formed to 'pacify' the Highlands of Scotland after the Jacobite rebellions; the name tells much about how the populace regarded it. Civil society was the antithesis of the military hierarchy of the coercive state.

Far from being the high priest of individualism venerated by modern commentators unfamiliar with his work, Smith was a communitarian. Smith's philosophical contribution was *The Theory of Moral Sentiments*. He asks readers to use their sympathetic imagination to see things from the perspectives of others – to become an 'impartial spectator'. My impartiality requires not detachment – I owe more to my neighbour's child than to the anonymous Bengalis – but rather renunciation of the selfishness which for Rawls is offset only by my ignorance about my role in the future society. Smith's impartial spectator, unlike the person behind Rawls's veil of ignorance, is fully cognizant of his actual role in present society, and his device of the impartial spectator draws 'me' to 'we'.

Smith saw no contradiction between the arguments of *The Wealth of Nations* (1776) and those of *The Theory of Moral Sentiments*. The relations of the market were always *relationships between people*. While Mrs Smith conversed with the baker and butcher (the sage never married and his mother kept house for almost all his life), Adam chatted with David Hume, Ferguson and the community of intellectuals which distinguished the Edinburgh society of his time. In Smith's world, we may pursue our own interest – not least because we understand it better than others – but not at the expense of others. The butcher trades as a butcher, but in doing so he does not cease to be a human being enmeshed in a web of obligations.

Thus communitarian ideas were present at the birth of economics. It has been a misfortune that after Smith's death, whereas his ideas on the butcher as tradesman inflated into Economic Man, a creature he would have abhorred, his ideas on the butcher as a person, and the good society as a harmony of sentiments, were largely forgotten.[*]

THE EVOLUTION OF COMMUNITARIAN THOUGHT

Eighteenth-century communitarianism was not unique to the salons of Edinburgh. The Irish writer and politician Edmund Burke wrote that 'To be attached to the subdivision, to love the little platoon we belong to in society, is the first principle (the germ as it were) of public affections. It is the first link in the series by which we proceed towards a love to our country, and to mankind.'[3]

In the early nineteenth century, Georg Hegel refined the idea of civil society, *bürgerliche Gesellschaft* or *Zivilgesellschaft*, as the link between the family and the state.[4] The French aristocrat Alexis de Tocqueville observed in *Democracy in America* that 'Americans of all ages, all stations of life, and all types of disposition are forever forming associations . . . In democratic countries knowledge of how to combine is the mother of all other forms of knowledge;

---

[*] Jesse Norman's fine book on Smith (Norman, 2018), which follows his earlier biography of Burke, redresses the balance.

on its progress depends that of all the others.'[5] And Karl Marx asserted that 'In the social production of their life, men enter into definite relations that are indispensable and independent of their will; these relations of production correspond to a definite stage of development in material forces of production. The sum total of these relations of production constitutes the economic structure of society.'[6]

The beginnings of modern communitarian thought are widely attributed to the Oxford philosopher Elizabeth Anscombe's 1958 article 'Modern Moral Philosophy',* but a major revival occurred in the 1980s. According to one proponent, Amitai Etzioni:

> Communitarianism is a social philosophy that . . . emphasizes the importance of society in articulating the good . . . Communitarians examine the ways shared conceptions of the good are formed, transmitted, justified, and enforced. Hence, their interest in communities (and moral dialogues within them), the historical transmission of values and mores, and the societal units that transmit and enforce values – such as the family, schools, and voluntary associations (including places of worship), which are all parts of communities.[7]

Etzioni was one of a group of thinkers who described communitarianism while conspicuously failing to form a community themselves. Prominent members were Alasdair MacIntyre, C. B. Macpherson, Michael Sandel, Charles Taylor and Michael Walzer. The doyen of modern American pragmatist philosophers, Richard Rorty, is also commonly grouped among communitarians.

EVOLUTION AND ECONOMIC MAN

For almost a century after Darwin, it was believed that evolution favoured Economic Man: the greedy and selfish would successfully push others aside in the competition for food, shelter and mates. Such

---

* Anscombe's article inspired a revival of virtue ethics and communitarianism developed as one of its strands.

survival of the fittest is true of nearly all mammalian species. Many humans are familiar with the greedy and selfish cat. Paul now thinks of his own specimen Grissou as *Cattus Economicus*.

The better understanding of evolutionary processes which began in the 1960s, and the recent development of evolutionary psychology, have told a different story. Humans have become successful not by being selfish and smart, but by being social. In well-functioning societies, humans construct and abide by a vast web of kindness and mutual obligations of which Economic Man would be incapable. As summed up by the evolutionary biologist Nicholas Christakis: 'humans everywhere are pre-wired to make a particular kind of society – one full of love, friendship, cooperation, and learning.'[8] (A notorious video demonstrates that some of his students had managed to resist their pre-wiring.)[9]

We (with some exceptions) have evolved to enjoy sociality and to be prosocial. Humans crave to belong to a group, and to value the good opinion of others in the group. (That at least was evident in the video.) We are prepared to forgo individual material rewards in pursuit of belonging and esteem. We seek not just the esteem of others – we want to be loved – but self-esteem – what Smith described as wanting 'to be *deserving* of love'. In the process, we become morally load-bearing – able to accept and abide by obligations that change how we behave. The genes which promote success are those which make us successful in a group. The resolution of the long-standing debates about nature versus nurture and group versus individual selection is that they are all inextricably linked.

And yet there is a problem, which Paul's cat exemplifies – the benefits of being the selfish member of a group working for some common purpose that benefits all its members. The feral cat is individualistic, greedy and selfish, but cannot shirk: it needs to hunt for its food. The domestic cat can be not just greedy and selfish, but also lazy. And Grissou is all these things. She can enjoy all the benefits of elaborate cooperative human activity – the perils endured by deep-sea cod fishermen, the investments of salmon farmers and the interacting efforts of canners, packers and supermarket supply chains which fill a can of Felix. No other species has implemented a food chain remotely as complex. And Grissou waits for Paul to open the can and place it's contents in her bowl – without ever contributing more than a grudging meow. She inhabits a world of rights without obligations, of both having tinned cat food and eating it – *an aristocat*.

Successful human groups pursuing a common purpose cannot permit aberrant members to ignore that purpose in favour of their own priorities. And they do not. They punish 'free-riders' – people who take the benefits of cooperative activity without contributing to them. Even the traders who manipulated LIBOR and other financial markets around the financial crisis sent emails to each other using phrases such as 'I owe you one.' Within their own group, they acknowledged webs of reciprocity and obligation even as they stole from the general public. One experimental approach to measuring pro-sociality invites students to make contributions to a pot for the benefit of all. The many similar experiments which have been conducted since repeatedly show that most people have a concept of fairness. They contribute to common pools and they agree to share even when given the option of keeping all for themselves.

But the authors of one early (1981) study entitled their paper 'Economists Free Ride: Does Anyone Else?' They observed, 'More than one-third of the economists either refused to answer the question regarding what is fair, or gave very complex, uncodeable responses. It seems that the meaning of "fairness" in this context was somewhat alien for this group.'[10] And the average contribution of economics graduate students was less than half of that of students as a whole. Perhaps economics trains students, not to understand economics, but to become Economic Men.

DO WE 'KNOW THE MODEL'?

Under the assumptions of market fundamentalism, everyone 'knows the model'. Cats *do* 'know the model' in the sense that they understand the pertinent aspects of their world sufficiently that they know what to do. When Grissou is hungry she looks up imploringly and says 'meow'; for much of the day she curls up in a cupboard out of the way of the dog. She 'knows the model' because her world is simple. But our world is not simple and we do not know the model.

Instead we experiment – we explore the world through trial and error, as Grissou did as a kitten. Play is natural to most young animals, but humans have evolved a distinctive capacity for *imaginative and creative* play. Squirrels are brilliant at climbing trees, and storing nuts, but in millions of years, no young squirrel appears to have thought, 'I want to live a different life,' and experimented in it. Being able to imagine alternative scenarios, some of which are better than our own, and to experiment with how to achieve them, is the foundation for our innate sense of *creative aspiration*. But our imagination leaps ahead of our creativity, hence the lament of frustrated geeks: 'We wanted flying cars, instead we got 140 characters.'[11]

Often, that creative imagination will take us into circumstances we do not fully understand, with negative as well as positive consequences: nuclear bombs, climate change. We need to be resilient and evolutionary biology reveals the required characteristics for a species to survive: widely distributed centres of decision that provide duplication and alternative sources of information and supply, so that, even if some of them are destroyed, the whole can continue to function. Modularity and redundancy are critical to the resilience of complex systems, and one of the lessons of the coronavirus crisis is that investment in these, even if it appears inefficient in the short term, is the key to sustainability in the long run.

But there are other, equally important, advantages of decentraliztion. Chapter 5 described the repeated failures of a single authority which planned on too large a scale and failed to learn quickly, or at all, from its failures. Human evolution has shaped us to imitate and to learn from each other. To learn, we need many experiments, and so creative initiative must be distributed. Joe Henrich, evolutionary biologist at Harvard, identifies collective intelligence as 'the secret of our success' as a species. The accumulation of collective intelligence is the combined product of competition and cooperation. The collective experience of a community is shared and stored, and this stock of knowledge transmitted through culture and education. That collective intelligence has gradually expanded, enabling us to create the complexity from which Grissou benefits but which she cannot comprehend. Henrich observes that young apes solve problems as swiftly as children: what they *cannot* do is learn from each other.

Although our collective intelligence has become more extensive, increasing complexity has placed such demands upon it that our understanding of the world pertinent to our purposes has diminished. Tacit knowledge – the knowledge that can be gained only from experience – becomes more important relative to codifiable knowledge which you can learn from a textbook. Since tacit knowledge is widely dispersed, decision-making authority should also be widely dispersed. And, as knowledge from lived experience becomes more important, self-realization by the inexperienced young becomes more vulnerable to tragedy.

COMMUNICATION FOR COMMON PURPOSE

Communities are both the nexus of mutuality and the storehouse of our collective intelligence. A successful community needs to inculcate a sense of shared belonging to articulate a causal chain from common sacrifice and shared values to a better future, and to define criteria for bestowing good opinion on other members of the group. That package creates social pressure to comply with group obligations, and guides people how to judge themselves.

Each of these – the common identity, the shared purpose, the bestowal of approval – requires communication and persuasion. A community is a network of communication, but individually we can only know a limited number of people; only in small groups can everyone communicate with everyone else. As our purposes have become more ambitious, we have needed to cooperate in larger groups, and for this we need super-communicators – politicians, business executives, religious leaders and journalists – who do communicate with everyone. More subtly, we all need to know that these communicators are talking to all of us. This turns the messages into *common* knowledge: we all know that we all know the same things.

Such large communities become multilayered – networks of networks. They have the potential for the cooperation that shelters us from storms, while nurturing the competitive creativity of progress. But they also have a darker potential: without pluralism, cooperation can turn into the stagnation of parochialism and errors of groupthink. Without clear boundaries, competition can turn businesses into the destructive entities that market addictive drugs and political leaders into the violent aggressors of hate-filled nationalism.

Successful societies create institutions which both sustain pluralism and discipline it. How the vast communities of multilayered networks that comprise our modern societies can best do this is the subject of communitarian governance.

9

Communitarian Governance

'There can be no man until there are at least two men in communication.'

– John Macmurray, Persons in Relation, 1961

Good governance provides citizens with scope for their fulfilment. Aristotle's criteria of good government are still relevant today. Good government is not tyrannical – it is based on a rule of law which wins the consent of the citizen. Good government is robust to what we now call rent-seeking – resisting capture by sectional interests. And good government is just – its processes seek fairness between different citizens and groups of citizens. This is a world very different from the self-righteous narcissism of expressive individualism. And very different from the world of a politician or a civil servant confidently bent on maximizing a social welfare function based on the aggregate of the individual preferences of anyone, anywhere, who might ever live.

COMMUNITARIANS IN POLITICS

As we described in the previous chapter, communitarian thinking was developed by Burke, by Hegel, by Marx – founders of radically different political traditions. And, during the first half of the twentieth century, the political rhetoric of both left and right was communitarian, the left emphasizing solidarity, the right nationhood – sentiments by no means contradictory. Franklin Roosevelt would call on both purposes to fight the Depression and, with Churchill, would inspire both purposes to defeat fascism. The post-war consensus sought to maintain this communitarian consensus. The rise of individualism has gradually undermined that governance, but modern communitarian philosophers have sometimes had influence.

Tony Blair was much influenced by the little-known Scottish philosopher John Macmurray. Guided by Macmurray's ideas, Blair and his senior political adviser David Miliband flirted with communitarian concepts, talking of a 'stakeholder society'. But this strand of thought died when economic policy was largely left in the hands of Gordon Brown, who broadly speaking embraced a philosophy of market fundamentalism combined with tax and benefit policies designed to pick up the pieces. This scenario found a parallel in the coalition government after 2010: the orthodox fiscal austerity of George Osborne effectively overrode the communitarian 'big society' inclinations of David Cameron.

The personal political affiliations of communitarian thinkers ranged widely. MacIntyre began as a communist before converting to Catholicism, and Etzioni was a conservative moralist. The religious element in communitarianism has always been strong – Macmurray wrote of his anguished struggles with faith and ended his life as a Quaker, while Blair himself became a Catholic. Macpherson was a student of Harold Laski and a lifelong Marxist. The communitarian sociologist Norman Dennis practised what he preached: brought up in Sunderland, in the north of England, he returned there to live, teaching at Newcastle University and sitting as a Labour member of Sunderland Council. Deploring the erosion of the moral communities of his childhood, he published late in life under the aegis of the free-market Institute of Economic Affairs.

The communitarian philosopher Michel Sandel's lectures on justice are reportedly the most popular course at Harvard University, their online version so widely viewed as to attract the ire of professors at lesser institutions who fear a threat to their continued employment.* Ed Milliband, who led the Labour Party from 2010 to 2015, had

* A widely reported open letter to Sandel (2012) from the philosophy department at San José State University claimed that he 'was spearheading the creation of two social classes in academia'.

studied admiringly under him, was sympathetic to his thinking, and invited him to address the party's conference. And David Cameron's promotion of the 'Big Society', encouraged by his adviser Steve Hilton, was manifestly communitarian. But fiscal austerity after 2010 meant that the proposed transfer of responsibilities to the community was not matched by a transfer of the resources necessary to incubate the community organizations that could meet them.

BEYOND THE TRAGEDY OF THE COMMONS

We return to the work of Elinor Ostrom, the political scientist who was awarded a Nobel Prize in Economics for her studies of small communities which had built social conventions that had overcome the free-rider problem – the 'tragedy of the commons'.[1] While each society was different, she discovered that these conventions which avoided the 'tragedy' conformed to a pattern, and attempted to lay out principles of political organization for a community. David Sloan Wilson argues that Ostrom's principles are scalable – they work just as well in large communities as in small ones.[2] This is important, because we need to cooperate at many levels. Foundational communities are small – Burke's 'little platoons' – but for many purposes we need to work together, building common purpose among thousands, millions and perhaps – as in fighting pandemics – even billions of people. This capacity for multilevel governance was indeed one of her principles.

Ostrom's most fundamental requirement was *boundedness*: clarity as to who belonged to the community and who did not. People could join the community, but common purpose could only develop if everyone knew to whom they owed obligations and from whom they could expect them. Citizens of a country recognize obligations to fellow citizens that are greater than those they owe to non-citizens and, correspondingly, citizens have greater rights to national resources than do non-citizens. That is what people mean by citizenship and why it matters. Civic nationalism is not ethnic nationalism.

It should hardly be controversial to say that the British government has duties to UK citizens which are not owed to people in the rest of the world. Boundedness does not mean 'keep out' in the style of Rousseau, but it does mean that the pace of new entry must be one with which members of the community are comfortable. And that entrants understand that they incur an obligation to become active members of the community through understanding and accepting that web of reciprocity of which they are becoming a part.

But Ostrom also emphasized empowerment. Community members should be able to participate in modifying the rules as circumstances change: and we can expect that in a world of radical uncertainty they will change in ways we cannot predict. Outsiders must respect these rule-making rights of community members. The community is in control of its rules, which are not imposed by outsiders or invented by a caste of lawyers based on imagined universalist norms which are deduced independently of the practices of the community in which they live.

Having set rules for common purpose, members of the community must enforce them, monitoring each other and using graduated sanctions when they are breached. When disputes arise, they need to be resolved through processes that are accessible and inexpensive, and which search for compromise.

The nature of the common purpose should determine which level of community is appropriate to deliver it. Some purposes require very high levels of common action, such as the defence of a nation, and a few need it to be global, such as addressing pandemic viruses. Others are more appropriate for a firm – supplying bread; or for a family – raising children; or for a city – building a metro. The guiding principle is subsidiarity: common purpose should be built and delivered through the lowest level at which cooperation is necessary.

PROTECTING AND BOUNDING PLURALISM AND COMPETITION

Humans are naturally creative, but creativity can only flourish in a community that accepts a diversity of ideas. If the only person permitted original ideas is the leader, the society risks the grim fate of China's Mao: mass starvation due to his tragically misnamed 'Great

Leap Forward'. The protection of pluralism requires that individuals should be able to think and express new thoughts, free of intimidation by either state or activists. Many new ideas no longer spring from an individual mind but from teams of people working together. Effective organizations, public and private, are designed to support both diversity within teams and diversity between teams. The antithesis of the National Bread Service.

New ideas come both from the codified knowledge derived from research and the practitioner knowledge from learning-by-doing. A good structure of communitarian governance gives voice to both explicit and tacit knowledge: knowing *that* and knowing *how*, each enhancing the other. Currently, we are far from that, with an academic community which mainly talks to itself and a wider community which, in Michael Gove's appalling phrase, has had enough of experts.

But diversity of opinion must itself be bounded to protect the capacity to cooperate. Pluralism of view is essential but must be disciplined. Communities need at some stage to move on from debate. The effective mediating leadership of community seeks consensus, but the search for consensus must not give any minority – whether greedy bankers or environmental activists – a veto over common purpose. And it certainly should not allow any minority to prevent the realization of a common purpose, whether by pulling down the global financial system or by obstructing airports. The ability to act with common purpose is one of the defining features of a successful community, valuable both for the progress that delivers good times and the shelter that protects us during bad ones.

Competition and pluralism go hand in hand; competition is both a consequence of pluralism and a spur to it. And the competitive drive gives a boost to innovation and effort which benefits the community as well as the competitor. So competition needs to be preserved. Often, the easiest way to maintain success is to inhibit rivals. Companies lobby government for protection from 'unfair' competition; political incumbents try to handicap challengers through strategies such as gerrymandering. A successful community builds institutions which guard against these erosions of pluralism. And resists attempts to emasculate them.[3]

But competition also needs to be bounded. Businesses not only need purpose beyond profit: not all business purposes should be legitimate. Businesses should not make profits by generating problems for society. The team of brilliant mathematicians which makes fortunes for its members by outwitting the managers of pension funds is a social parasite, not a role model.[4] Political majorities should never use their power of common action to abuse minorities. The boundary between competition to outperform and cooperation to predate is not usually difficult to draw.

LEVELS OF TRUST

Communities, like dinghies, may have more than one locally stable outcome. There is an unhappy outcome – the dinghy is upside down and the participants cling to the edges. This is locally *very* stable – once upside-down, it takes a great effort, involving simultaneous cooperative activity from many participants, to correct it. Typically, the collective intelligence of dysfunctional societies is backward-looking and divided, with each group wrongly attributing failure to some other group within the society. Discussion is focussed on whose fault it is that the dinghy overturned rather than how to turn it the right way up. These damaging ideas result in further failure which is misinterpreted as confirming evidence of fault.

A successful community is like the upright, well-crewed dinghy: it can keep sailing to where its occupants want to go. But the upright dinghy may be less stable than the capsized one. Puffs of wind and large waves can overturn it, so that frequent small adjustments are needed from the helmsman and crew. It is easier to destroy a successful community than to build one.

And where do we find those successful communities? There are many surveys of the state of Robert Putnam's 'social capital' across the world; one of the longest standing is the World Values Survey, which among many other questions asks whether people generally feel they can trust others. It is easy to identify the upright dinghies – the smaller countries of the developed world. Scandinavian nations always come out well. And these countries also have high per capita incomes, low inequality, top the surveys of reported well-being, and perform well on other social indicators such as low rates of crime and teenage pregnancy and infrequency of resort to the courts.[5] There is no single direction of causality: the ideas, the economic outcomes and the governance of the polity are intricately interdependent.

But there are also craft that are upside-down, dysfunctional societies in which people have little trust in other people or in institutions and where the principal aspiration of many of the able and enterprising is to live somewhere else. And then there are failed states, for which we cannot even collect data. Some countries lie in between. On 'Can you trust other people?', Britain and the United States are well above Colombia and Zimbabwe, but well below Norway and New Zealand. And some Asian countries score highly on trust in people but poorly on trust in institutions.

One study tested for pro-sociality in sixteen widely different societies.[6] Pro-sociality – as seen in Copenhagen and Melbourne – meant not just a high level of willingness to sacrifice for the public good, but a willingness to impose penalties on free-riders even at some cost to oneself. But in other cities, in Riyadh and Athens, for example, not only was the dinghy upside-down, but people were ready to keep it there. Respondents not only did not punish free-riders, but actually punished those who sacrificed for the public good. This wide variation between the societies was correlated with the rule of law: the communitarian societies, such as Denmark, were also the most law-abiding. So community and state were not alternatives: with the state reduced to its proper role, state and community were complementary.

COMMUNICATION FOR COMMON PURPOSE

In the animal kingdom many species have evolved leaders, but their style of leadership is always dominance. Humans belong to the animal kingdom, so we have inherited an instinct for leadership by dominance. And authoritarian hierarchy can work well when humans are engaged in tribal battles, as with Winston Churchill's war leadership, or General Wade's command of the Black Watch. But Adam Ferguson had understood that the requirements of a civil society with multiple objectives and facing radical uncertainty were very different.

Many political and business leaders delude themselves into believing that they are of the calibre of Churchill, or aspire to the untrammelled power conferred on Wade. In our age of individualism, the dominant leader uses coercion – rewards and penalties linked to scrutiny – and ties them to the behaviour he wants. He (rarely she) is the 'commander-in-chief'.

But you can't even run a modern army that way. To build common purpose, humans don't need commanders-in-chief: the form of leadership best suited to coping with the challenges of radical uncertainty is distinctive. We need super-communicators, or communicators-in-chief. Humans, *and only humans*, have evolved a style of leadership by *persuasion* rather by *instruction*. Effective persuasion rests upon trust and the good opinion of other members of the group. Trust is won not by what leaders say, but what they do.

Actions enable a leader to establish credibility of purpose through personal sacrifice. Joe Henrich describes the behaviour of such leaders as 'prosocial, generous, and cooperative . . . using self-deprecating humour'.[7] An effective leader communicates by combining credibility-enhancing actions with language that specifies complex meanings. The combination is vital: leaders always have the power to be heard, but only credibility can convert what is heard into what is accepted.

As we are plunged into unpredicted catastrophes, we need good leaders to build the common purpose that copes with them. Nicholas Christakis assembled evidence from a natural experiment: shipwrecks in which the stranded crew needed to collaborate to survive. In similar situations some succeeded, others perished. Self-sacrificing leaders such as Ernest Shackleton earned respect and enabled almost all his crew to survive the most appalling privation in the Antarctic. Our age of individualism is epitomized by Francesco Schettino, the captain of the *Costa Concordia*, a cruise ship wrecked a few miles from the coast of Italy in 2012, resulting in thirty deaths. Schettino had the good fortune to 'fall into' a lifeboat, leaving 300 passengers on board.* Humans are naturally both cooperative and

* His ludicrous account was insufficiently convincing: he was convicted and jailed.

competitive. Shackleton successfully harnessed cooperation in the face of adversity while Schettino was successful in the competition to reach the lifeboat first. Shackleton came from a naval culture in which the captain went down with his ship; Schettino from a country led at the time by Silvio Berlusconi, the pioneer of self-indulgent narcissism in politics.

When John F. Kennedy was inaugurated as President of the United States in January 1961, he was the youngest ever elected holder of the office. Within three months, the CIA presented to him a plan to invade Cuba and overthrow Fidel Castro, the firebrand who had ousted dictator Fulgencio Batista two years earlier. The invasion was to be disguised as a coup by elements of the Cuban military with support from exiled opponents of the regime. The outcome was a fiasco. The exiles who had been landed with the assistance of the US Navy were quickly rounded up and killed or jailed.

The American psychologist Irving Janis popularized the term 'groupthink' for the process by which a group arrives at a bad decision because of the unwillingness or inability of its members to challenge the prevailing narrative.[8] One of Janis's signature examples was the proceedings which led to the approval of the Bay of Pigs landings. After the event, the Joint Chiefs of Staff said that they had had reservations about the invasion plan but had felt inhibited in expressing their misgivings because they did not reflect the prevailing narrative of US supremacy. A new and inexperienced President presided over meetings in which challenge to that narrative was discouraged.

Kennedy learned from that experience, and was determined not to repeat it. His predecessor as President, Dwight Eisenhower, framed the key post-mortem question, asking Kennedy: 'Mr. President, before you approved this plan did you have everybody in front of you debating the thing so you got pros and cons yourself and then made your decision?'[9] When Cuba again became the principal issue on the presidential agenda, Kennedy managed the process of decision-making in a very different way, consciously promoting pluralism among his advisers. He did this by establishing two groups which were told to write papers to support their preferred option, and then to exchange documents and critique each other's narrative.[10] He also decided not to attend all their meetings. He did not want his presence to prompt the attendees to second-guess what he wanted to hear. He wanted to know what they really thought. As Robert Kennedy, his brother and Attorney General, later wrote, 'the fact that we were able to talk, debate, argue, disagree, and then debate some more was essential in choosing our ultimate course . . . Opinion, even fact itself, can best be judged by conflict, by debate.'[11]

Leaders such as Berlusconi and Trump are overconfident in taking decisions because they are temperamentally overconfident about everything. Technocratically inclined leaders such as Gordon Brown and Emmanuel Macron who believe that they 'know the model' are similarly overconfident in their abilities to design strategy. All miss the importance of bottom-up tacit knowledge and are prone to bully because they interpret disagreement as insubordination rather than an opportunity to learn from the knowledge of others and the clash of differing opinions.

In contrast, a good communitarian leader starts from modesty: such leaders accept that they do not know how to achieve many of the common purposes that are their goals. That element of humility characterized great business leaders, typically little known to a general public, such as Alfred Sloan, who built General Motors into the world's largest car manufacturer, overtaking the one overseen by the autocratic Henry Ford. Or Bill Allen, who achieved the same for Boeing in civil aviation, or the pharmaceutical executives George Merck and R. W. Johnson. These leaders inspired their workers with a shared sense of common purpose – a purpose which was to build a great business, rather than to maximize shareholder value, although one consequence of committed teamwork was that all these companies did create a great deal of value, including value for shareholders. Such leaders decentralize many decisions to practitioners who have the tacit knowledge garnered from experience, while providing resources to develop the codified knowledge of experts. They ensure that expert knowledge is available to the practitioners, and facilitate the sharing of practitioner experience. The good communitarian leader does not aim to become the source or conduit of all wisdom, but rather to expand the scope of collective knowledge.

Once established, forward-looking common purpose reinforces shared identity: 'we' are the people who are jointly performing the purpose. As the strategy succeeds, it validates the need for sacrificing self-interest: all benefit from collective knowledge and achievement, enhancing trust both in the narrative on which action has been based and in other members of the community. In consequence, a successful communitarianism is robust.

All societies have the potential for such common purpose – it harnesses the unique capacity of human beings to be morally load-bearing. But such happy outcomes are not inevitable. Upright dinghies can capsize if those onboard are negligent.

10

Communitarian Politics

*'Democracy shows not only its power in reforming govern-
ments, but in regenerating a race of men and this is the greatest blessing of free governments.'*

– Andrew Jackson[1]

The state is not the only entity capable of meeting common purposes.
But it is an essential one, so the process by which it is controlled is
vital. States are controlled through politics, but politics has been contaminated by the rise of individualism. The traditional left–right axis
no longer describes current allegiances as revealed by voting patterns
and values. Membership of political parties has declined dramatically
and the residue is dominated by minorities unrepresentative of the
supporters of their parties. On the right, the business interest frets
about tax burdens and excessive regulation; on the left, moral superiority frets about the NHS, refugees and climate.

Too frequently, single-issue pressure groups driven by 'activists'
have replaced pragmatic coalitions, while 'activism' has come to
mean 'drawing attention' – ostensibly to the chosen issue, but in practice, perhaps most especially *to oneself*: '*I* care about this.' Energy is
expended in noisy expression of individual self-righteousness, rather
than in encouraging effective collective solutions to problems. The
activist left denounces austerity as 'social murder', repeating claims
that it led to over 100,000 preventable deaths; the activist right publicly gloats at its victory over the 'remoaners' who make up nearly half
the country. This kind of exchange of abuse is relished by the extremes,

but it is ugly and damages our social fabric. Democratic politics does not need to be the exchange of school-playground insults, and when it becomes that, democracy itself is threatened. Democratic politics tends more naturally towards the centre. But communitarian politics is more than centrist. Although it encourages moderation and compromise, it seeks to unite people around a shared purpose rather than to secure agreement by offending no one.

COMMUNITIES, INDIVIDUALS, STATES AND COURTS

Instead of building common purpose in a community, individualism, both philosophical and economic, focusses on the clash of individual interests, which may and too often do take the form of tradeable property rights in which the richest bid ahead of opposing interests, or rights of entitlement in which the assertive triumph over the meek.

Every family experiences and manages incompatible individual interests. But we conjecture that not even in the Becker household did the parties use either legal processes or markets to resolve their differences. We cannot be sure: 'marriage is no exception and can be successfully analyzed within the framework provided by modern economics,'[2] Becker wrote in an article published between the death of his first wife and his second marriage. 'If correct,' he continued, 'this is compelling additional evidence on the unifying power of economic analysis.' But it is not correct. Households get along, making compromises as necessary to secure amicable and cooperative living. Interests are mediated by mechanisms which are in the broadest sense political processes.

And mediation and cooperation which facilitate benefit from the growth of collective knowledge does not only take place in households. Communitarians recognize that there are many levels of mutuality, such as families and firms, churches and localities, and nations. Each association is a network within which narratives sustain a collective intelligence. A person belongs to several such communities and our motivations are largely shaped by these collective intelligences. And these communities develop a 'harmony of sentiments' which enables them to mediate possible conflicts.

Individualism and echo chambers erode these mechanisms of community association, and their erosion has been extensive in Britain. Privatization has created an astonishing range of new property rights. Regional water boards became companies with complex and obscure ownership structures. The Land Registry – well, do you know the legal status of the Land Registry, which records your title to any land you think you own?* 'The Hydro', the astonishingly well-loved agency which had brought electricity to the rural north of Scotland, is now the faceless SSE plc.

And community-based organizations became – something else. Trade unions dwindled, and the most successful became lobbies for the interests of overprotected public sector employees. Mutual building societies were converted into failed banks. The cooperative movement, for long a beacon of community-based trading, fell victim to spectacular mismanagement. Partnerships, which had been the norm in activities such as investment banking and estate agency, were transformed into limited companies. And lawyers formed private-equity-backed businesses which sent you texts about the hypothetical accident that wasn't your fault.

Other lawyers established firms of solicitors and chambers of barristers to pursue more and more imaginative assertions of human rights. And further legal interference carelessly dismantled the most important communitarian mechanism of welfare provision. Many thousands of defined benefit pension schemes had been built up over the post-war decades, providing secure standards of living in retirement for millions of people. Those covering around half the population rapidly collapsed once foolishly drafted new regulations reinterpreted the undertakings made by these schemes as legal rights and demanded evidence that these obligations could be fulfilled with certainty. That made their liabilities too onerous for firms to accept in an inherently uncertain world.

* It is a non-ministerial government department, accountable to UKGI, a company which is 100 per cent owned by the Treasury.

POLITICS AND THE COURTS

Well-structured communities, like all households outside the ambit of influence of the University of Chicago, move beyond clashes of interests through common purpose and compromise. But legal settlements have binary outcomes. As more and more interests have been reclassified as 'rights', the political domain of the courts has increased. In Britain, lawyers have encroached on what were formerly political decisions.[3] There are several factors at work here, but the most important are the rise of the culture of rights and the deliberate extension by judges of the scope of judicial review of administrative decisions. Lord Sumption, the recently retired Supreme Court justice who is the most distinguished British jurist of our time, has forcibly warned of the dangers these developments pose for both democracy and the rule of law.

Governments may often make bad decisions, but that does not make the courts the appropriate forum for reversing these decisions. Lady Hale, at the time President of the Supreme Court, recently made the extraordinary statement, quoted by Sumption, that 'the courts may be thought better qualified [to decide such matters than the legislature] because they are better able to weigh the evidence . . . in a dispassionate manner, *without the external pressures to which legislators may be subject* [authors' emphasis].' Lady Hale is right that the relevant abortion law in Northern Ireland was monstrous and that the Supreme Court is a more effective deliberative forum than the dysfunctional Northern Ireland Assembly. But that is not the point. Such weighing of evidence and assessment of the balance of argument is, in a democracy, a matter for political, not legal, determination. Contrary to Lady Hale, *subjecting legislators to external pressures is the very essence of democracy*.

Another unwise blurring of the lines between politics and law comes from the introduction of declaratory legislation, in which political aspirations are translated into 'legally binding' commitments. Such legislation has required governments to reduce budget deficits, eliminate child poverty and reduce net greenhouse-gas emissions. Of course, parliaments can legally unbind themselves as quickly as they can bind themselves, though they do so with less fanfare. The Fiscal Responsibility Act of 2010 was quietly repealed and the child-poverty objective legislated for in 2010 was simply ignored when it became clear that the 'legally binding' targets could not be met. We have until 2050 to see whether the climate-change objectives are achieved. But making the targets more stringent, raising the 2050 obligation to 100 per cent from 80 per cent, carries no cost in the foreseeable future. Similarly, in 2015 the Welsh government promoted a future well-being Act. Unsurprisingly, since Wales is the poorest region of mainland Britain, the first purpose was to 'develop a skilled and well-educated population in an economy which generates wealth and provides employment opportunities'. But this fine aspiration came without any strategy for achieving it. Concern for the economy has not inhibited it from cancelling the Newport bypass, a road project that would have addressed a long-standing complaint of Welsh business. Nor has concern for the environment inhibited it from buying and heavily subsidizing Cardiff airport.

It is good that governments make forward-looking commitments. But these should be undertakings *to citizens* in which difficult choices are navigated *through politics*. 'Legally binding' policy objectives are either ignored or hand to the courts the determination of the means of achieving them, a task for which they are ill equipped, but perhaps too willing to attempt.

Even by international legal standards, the adversarial nature of British courts with its win–lose outcomes is particularly poorly suited to resolving political issues. Lawyers are trained to exaggerate points of difference whereas political disputes need to be mediated by compromise. Antagonistic 'human rights' lawyers have proliferated when what we need are more mutually trusted mediators. The adversarial process is a contest in persuasion. The skill of being persuasive has consequently become valuable, and so court cases are often determined through *the market in persuasion*. The real loser in this process is the community.

Public prosecutors are well paid in comparison with others in public employment, but not relative to the lawyers opposing them in complex cases. And so the most persuasive lawyers are frequently working to defeat the public interest. The law has failed, where the public interest manifestly required it, to punish the bankers who lined their own pockets at shareholder and ultimately public expense. The *Financial Times* summarized the outcome of the unsuccessful prosecution of the only senior executives to be arraigned (for murky transactions designed to avert the necessity of a government stake in the company): 'In essence, the bank could not be held accountable for the actions of the chief executive, but neither could the chief executive be accountable for the actions of Barclays.'[4] Catch-22 as crafted by lawyers.

A danger in all of this is that *the more that the law encroaches on politics, the more politics encroaches on the law*. Constitutional constraints that limit the ability of governments to sacrifice fundamental long-term goals for reasons of short-term expediency are valuable. But if these constraints are too restrictive, they can become permanent locks on change. The radical uncertainty inherent in modernity delivers circumstances that could not have been anticipated. The US Constitution, written more than two centuries ago, is extensive and detailed. But it is not useful to speculate on what James Madison would have thought about regulating the internet. The sensible response has been flexible interpretation of its provisions: the same written words have been interpreted as implying different things at different times. But, in consequence, interpretation has become a political process. The US Supreme Court now regularly divides on the basis of partisan allegiance: despite the fancy robes, this is politics, not law. And so appointments to the Court are influenced primarily by the partisan allegiance of the President – who nominates – and the Senate – which must confirm – and only secondarily on legal distinction.

Legal constraints on political action are therefore best restricted to matters on which there is wide consensus, such as corruption and lying to the public, rather than trying to decide those essentially political matters for which compromise and pragmatism are necessary. Flexibility is one of the desirable features of a political system, but it is best not entrusted to the motivated reasoning of lawyers. We need to reset and clarify the boundaries of recourse to parliament, mediation and the courts.

DIRECT DEMOCRACY?

Direct democracy – the resolution of as many issues as possible by one person, one vote plebiscites – is another means of resolving conflicting interests. And technology has made it imaginable that such democracy could be implemented on a large scale.

British politics was historically hostile to such ideas. In 1945 Clement Attlee deposed, 'I could not consent to the introduction into our national life of a device so alien to all our traditions as the referendum which has only too often been the instrument of Nazism and fascism.'[5] Such direct democracy was introduced to Britain only in 1975: the first referendum on British membership of what was then the EEC was used by a Labour prime minister to resolve a split within his party. It was used for the same purpose in 2016, although the party was different, as was the result. In 2010 the Liberal Democrats secured a referendum on proportional representation, which they believed would give them more seats, as a condition for a coalition, while in 2011 the SNP demanded one on secession as a way of maintaining momentum after winning a majority in the Scottish parliament: hence, all four of the major parties had licensed a fundamental change in the nature of our democracy for a specific, and different, purpose-of-the-moment.

The two recent referendums – on Scotland and the European Union – both proved disastrously divisive. Such division is inevitable when the winning sides secure narrow majorities of 55 per cent and 52 per cent respectively. And the EU result handed to parliament the task of deciding what the result actually meant, a task which it proved unable to perform. If the Scottish referendum had produced a yes vote – implying a major change to the status quo – analogous problems would have emerged. Very few political issues reduce to simple yes/no choices.

REPRESENTATIVE DEMOCRACY

Effective democracy is representative. The most powerful exposition of representative democracy ever written, at its very beginnings, is

Burke's famous address to the electors of Bristol. 'Government and legislation are matters of reason and judgment not inclination,' he observed.[6] Voters, the authors included, do not have the information or expertise to determine foreign policies for the Middle East or environmental standards for London air; and nor do they have time or inclination to do so. They wisely seek trustworthy representatives who have or will acquire relevant expertise and knowledge or who can at least oversee the process of doing so; even the most conscientious parliamentarian can be well informed in only a few areas of policy. Passion should not be confused with expertise – there is an important difference between the shrill activist whose knowledge is based on briefings from the National Rifle Association or Greenpeace and the committee chair who masters a subject through exposure to a wide range of advice and information. The varieties of experiment in citizen assemblies, which attempt to give randomly selected groups the time and power to become properly informed on some specific policy issue and then seek their collective judgement – an example is the one recently used in Ireland – are an interesting innovation in democratic practice. They attempt to synthesize the tacit knowledge of community with the codified knowledge of expertise.

Burke continued, 'Your representative owes you, not his industry only, but his judgment; and he betrays, instead of serving you, if he sacrifices it to your opinion.'[7] The electors of Bristol did not much like Burke's judgements on matters such as trade, Catholic emancipation and American independence and did not re-elect him; however, most people would now agree that history proved him right on all these issues.

'Parliament is not a *congress* of ambassadors from different and hostile interests; which interests each must maintain, as an agent and advocate, against other agents and advocates; but parliament is a *deliberative* assembly of *one* nation, with *one* interest, that of the whole [original emphasis].'[8] It is Burke's notion of *one* interest – a common purpose – which a certain kind of individualism rejects. In the heyday of Thatcherism, a policy adviser said to one of the authors, 'Of course, there is no such thing as a collective interest, only a coincidence of individual interests.' We profoundly disagree: communitarian politics builds informed common purpose.

Burke's concept of a deliberative assembly is *not* one in which people begin speeches with 'Speaking as a woman of colour' or 'Speaking on behalf of the financial sector'. Or, 'My members in the National Union of Placemakers, or the Taxpayers Alliance, think that Placemaking is vital to the national economy, or that taxes are too high.' Nor one in which representatives see all issues through the lens of their effect on Borrioboola-Gha.

PARTY LEADERSHIP

Not only do we select representatives to work in parliament, studying the many issues on which they pass legislation that we have neither time nor inclination to know about, but, being physically proximate to the candidates for government office, they can observe much better than we can their strengths and weaknesses.

Enthusiasm for direct democracy led political parties to adopt systems for choosing party leaders which gave the choice to the membership rather than members of parliament. But abandoning representative democracy as the system for choosing party leaders led to a system that is far *less* representative. The election of Jeremy Corbyn as Labour leader in 2015 illustrates the two fundamental weaknesses of this mechanism of direct election. First, it favoured an individual who was, in the judgement of close colleagues, not capable of doing the job. Second, it empowered a group of activists much less attuned to the supporters and potential supporters of the party than the elected representatives of these supporters.

The move from election through representative democracy to election by paying party members radically reduces the size of the group enfranchised. Even in the 2020 Labour leadership election, with the party's expanded membership and heavy loss of seats, the 500,000 party members eligible to vote are only 10 per cent of the 5 million Labour supporters who voted for Labour's members of parliament.[9] A Conservative leadership election decided by members instead of the MPs representing Conservative voters in winning constituencies shrinks the electorate by 98 per cent.[10] Yet, more seriously, these shrinkages are not random. Shrinkage empowers the activist extremist 10 per cent (or 2 per cent) by disempowering the more moderate vast majority. Indeed, the opinions that the Labour Party most needed to hear were not those of its 500,000 activists, but the 2.5 million former Labour voters who had *not* voted for the party in 2019.

INCLUSIVE DEMOCRACY?

Politics should be *inclusive*, but what might that mean? We have already suggested that it means that leaders in Britain should be elected by their MPs, whose job is to represent their party's voters, rather than by small groups of party activists. But if we are to have truly *representative* MPs, they must be *representative*.

That is less and less the case. Increasingly, politicians are people who have had no experience outside politics. A common career path is to go from university into some apprentice role in research or support for established politicians or political groupings, to become a 'spad' (Special Adviser) to a minister and then to be selected for some constituency with whom he or she had no previous connection. Representativeness is also about 'lived experience'. As most parents discover, children drastically change your daily life. Yet until Boris Johnson, with several children, became Prime Minister, the recent leaders of all three of the largest countries in Europe had zero children in total. Maybe such skewed representation has some connection with Europe's demographic crisis.

The cultural and social gap between citizens and members of parliament is widest in working-class constituencies, such as Don Valley and Stoke North. When Herbert Morrison and Ernest Bevin were distinguished Cabinet ministers, voters not only in their constituencies but in other parts of the country could reasonably feel that they were represented by people who, despite their advancement, understood and had experienced the worlds these voters inhabited. And, in 1966, Don Valley was represented by a former miner, who was succeeded by another former miner and then by a local truck driver who had studied part-time for a degree from the University of Sheffield. Similarly, also in 1966, the member for Stoke North was John

Forrester, previously a schoolmaster in the town and a famously conscientious constituency MP; but he was deselected in 1985 at the time of extremist infiltration of many local Labour parties and replaced by a councillor from the London borough of Lambeth who had been disqualified from local public office.

CENTRALIZED GOVERNANCE?

Britain is the most highly centralized large country in the OECD. Both strategy design and its implementation have become increasingly handled from the top. When the European Commission provided 'Structural Funds' to help the poorest regions of Europe, the money for Britain's regions was required by Whitehall to be managed through one Whitehall authority – which consequently became by far the largest manager of EC funds in Europe. Due to such extreme centralization, manifest also in the centralization of testing for coronavirus, local governments in Britain have been deskilled. With little discretion, they cannot attract talent. In Germany, bright young public servants gravitate to public administration in their own region. In Britain, their aspiration is Whitehall. We need bright people not just in Whitehall, where they are too distant from practitioner experience, but in local government around the country.

Modernity plunges us into a world which we cannot fully understand and for which we need many organizations whose members strive together for some common purpose. As with business, politics needs organizations that are able both to compete and to collaborate. In politics, as in business, top-down management is fragile, starved of information derived from local knowledge, and demotivating for those who hold that local knowledge. The state is overloaded with obligations that it cannot fulfil and so loses trust and legitimacy.

PARTICIPATORY DEMOCRACY

As with 'inclusive', we can all agree that we want democracy to be 'participatory', but what should participation mean? We do not think it means frequent elections. We think that it means widespread opportunities to take part in the process of building well-informed, forward-looking common purpose, starting with small groups that feed into larger ones, as it does in Switzerland, probably the country with the most effective participatory democracy. That marriage of purpose with the knowledge necessary to guide it is essential but uneasy: the passionate want to shut out the ambiguities often consequent upon knowledge, and the experts are often repelled by the cavalier style of the passionate. Decentralization is essential to such participation – people build mutual trust by meeting each other face to face. But so is collaboration in generating and sharing expertise. Ideas initially coalesce within each group, flow up so as to be compared and synthesized, and then flow down again, enabling the many initial sources of knowledge to become common. Such a process has its tensions and frictions but is the means through which common purpose develops.

Participation matters in several ways. It draws tacit information from experience and so provides an early-warning system for the flaws inevitable in a world of radical uncertainty. Participation enables people to contribute to decisions and their implementation, and so reduces the problem of compliance: people own the decisions and so are more willing to honour them. And finally, by taking part in a common endeavour, people bond, forging the mutual trust that is a vital asset of a successful society. Belonging is so important to humans that they often want to participate in a common endeavour even if it has no other purpose than commonality. Performative rituals are widespread: they are pure and enjoyable expressions of mutuality.[11] The ideal rituals bond across the political divides – football, *The Great British Bake Off* and clapping for the NHS. We need weaker bonding to political identities – fewer ritual denunciations of adversaries – and stronger bonding to shared identities, of which living in the same place is the most obvious. Given the need to decentralize political decisions from Whitehall to localities, place-based bonding is also uniquely valuable. Fewer national political rallies chanting slogans of denunciation, and more festivals celebrating place.

But participatory democracy is not just instrumentally useful for societal well-being: it is existentially vital. The point is well illustrated by the opportunities and dangers posed by artificial intelligence and

Big Data. Whatever the future capabilities of machines, they cannot be morally load-bearing because humans are self-aware and mortal, whereas machines are not. Machines can be used not only to complement and enhance human decision-making, but for bad: search optimization has already morphed into influence-optimization. We must keep morally pertinent decision-taking firmly in the domain of humanity.[12]

An informed, participatory democracy built on mutuality comes with mundane responsibilities as well as great ones. But in meeting such practical obligations – in accepting the agency of being morally load-bearing – we end up with a better society. And in our mutual efforts to be morally purposive, not only do we reap a better society, we may each find peace of mind.

I I

Communitarianism, Markets and Business

> 'In a knowledge economy, a good business is a community
> with a purpose, not a piece of property.'
>
> – Charles Handy

The dominant account of business in society in recent decades has been one that is both repulsive and false. Repulsive because it fails to distinguish the motives of businesspeople from those of a criminal gang: if this were indeed what motivated the people who work in the private sector, the public sector employees, largely left-leaning, would be fully justified in their sense of moral superiority. But this account is false – working together to deliver goods and services which people want is what most corporations actually do, and it is that common purpose which provides satisfying and rewarding employment. Just as most people in the public sector are working for some purpose larger than their paycheck, so are most people in the private sector. They are mostly doing tasks that are no less useful to society, and no better paid, than those in the public sector. The main difference is security: the public sector cannot go bankrupt, much of its workforce still enjoys pension terms that are guaranteed, ultimately by the state's power to tax the private sector, and it remains heavily unionized. There is no basis for a sense of moral superiority among those who work in it.

COLLECTIVE KNOWLEDGE

Humans collectively know far more than any individual could imagine knowing. Our capacity to draw on this collective knowledge is the secret of our success as a species. No individual knows how to fly, and no individual knows how to build an aeroplane. But a community of 10,000 people working together do.

An Airbus is one of the most complex products of human intelligence. Wings and landing gear are made in the UK. The tail wings and communication systems are made in Germany. The rear fuselage is manufactured in Spain. Final assembly is in Toulouse, and the forward fuselage is also manufactured in France, along with some components for the wings and radar. A custom set of barges, ships and trolleys, to allow for roll-on roll-off movement of the components, is used to get the components to Toulouse. The Airbus consortium came into being as a combination of the different capabilities of different European firms, which eventually merged their operations into a single corporate entity.

No single person could command even a fraction of the skills and knowledge to build an Airbus or to fly from London to Sydney. The outcome is only possible as a result of a very large number of people working together. Human intelligence is collective intelligence, and the ability to construct a complex artefact such as a commercial aircraft is the product of a collective intelligence built up over more than 200 years. The tens of thousands of people who have contributed to every Airbus flight do not know who the other contributors are; they communicate in small groups which in turn communicate with other small groups. To see economic life from any perspective other than that of the group is severely limiting – indeed to miss the central point of how modern business functions.

MODULARITY

This modularity is fundamental to the modern economy. Effective economic, social and political organizations are, like Airbus, formed from the building blocks of smaller cooperating units. They are hierarchical, to be sure, but effective hierarchies are structured from the bottom up and not simply imposed from the top down.

The decision theorist (and winner of the Nobel Prize in Economics) Herbert Simon illustrated the power of modularity with a parable:

There once were two watchmakers, named Hora and Tempus, who made very fine watches. The phones in their workshops rang frequently and new customers were constantly calling them. However, Hora prospered while Tempus became poorer and poorer. In the end, Tempus lost his shop. What was the reason behind this?

The watches consisted of about a thousand parts each. The watches that Tempus made were designed such that when he had to put down a partly assembled watch, it immediately fell into pieces and had to be reassembled from the basic elements. Hora had designed his watches so that he could put together sub-assemblies of about ten components each, and each sub-assembly could be put down without falling apart. Ten of these sub-assemblies could be put together to make a larger sub-assembly, and ten of the larger sub-assemblies constituted the whole watch.[1]

Simon's example was developed by Arthur Koestler, who described 'holarchy', a concept which he derived from the South African Jan Smuts.[*] Both elaborated the idea that any organism – biological or social – is built from modules, 'holons', which have an independent character but in total add to more than the sum of the parts. The human body functions through multiple interacting organs – heart, lungs, kidneys. And Smuts put his thinking into important practice in helping to create the League of Nations, then the United Nations, and the British Commonwealth. A clearer understanding of Smuts's concept of holons might have clarified debate about the nature of the European Union both for devotees of a European superstate and members of UKIP.

Sadly, this language has been appropriated by new-age philosophy.[†] The shoe retailer Zappos, owned by an atypically tolerant Amazon, claims to practice 'holacracy', by which it appears to mean having no

---

[*] Both Koestler and Smuts were remarkable polymaths – the former one of the few novelists and critics to have been sentenced to death and live to write about it, the other at different times barrister, general, statesman and philosopher – but each with a dark side: Koestler was a sexual predator, Smuts, like almost all Afrikaaners of his time, an incorrigible racist.
[†] If you google 'holistic' you will be directed to a lengthy list of practitioners of alternative medicine.

formal management structure at all, but simply hoping that groups of cooperative individuals will come together to get things done. Holacracy was fashionable among other Silicon Valley companies for a time, but with little enduring impact. The internet publisher Medium, which once had made a similar claim to holacracy, abandoned it after a three-year trial. As Andy Doyle, its head of operations, said, 'For us, it was getting in the way of work.'[2] Business organization requires both pluralism and discipline.

MEDIATING HIERARCHY

The cooperative ethos of self-organizing teams has proved an effective means of promoting employee motivation in many organizations. It was how the East India Company colonized large parts of Asia in the eighteenth century, when messages from head office took eight weeks to arrive. It was how nineteenth-century coal mines and shipyards became productive. It was how in the twentieth century Japanese car manufacturers secured product quality unobtainable on assembly lines. And how in the twenty-first century Apple, Google and Microsoft would dominate the internet.

But some hierarchy is necessary for any organization in which decisions are to be made and implemented. As Simon's example forcibly reminds us, a watch does not assemble itself through spontaneous order, and even Zappos does not deliver shoes that way. Formal structures are required to create a complex artefact or coordinate a complex organization. Margaret Blair and Lynn Stout describe the modern business as *mediating hierarchy*:

> A public corporation is a team of people who enter into a complex agreement to work together for their mutual gain. Participants . . . yield control over outputs and key inputs (time, intellectual skills, or financial capital) to the hierarchy. They enter into this mutual agreement in an effort to reduce wasteful shirking and rent-seeking by relegating to the internal hierarchy the right to determine the division of duties and resources in the joint enterprise. They thus agree not to specific terms or

outcomes (as in a traditional 'contract'), but to participate in a process of internal goal setting and dispute resolution.[3]

Two features of this account deserve particular emphasis. Blair and Stout do not prioritize any particular group of stakeholders. The mediating hierarchy – and ultimately its chief executive and board of directors – can and must 'determine the division of duties and resources in the joint enterprise'. This is an approach wholly different from the 'nexus of contracts' theory, or the view of the firm which sees a cascade of principal-agent contracts reporting to the shareholders. Of course, in a corporation, the shareholders collectively have the power to change the directors or sack the chief executive if they do not like the division of duties and resources which has been implemented – a right which is sometimes, in extremis, exercised. Just as the employees have the right to leave, and the customers and suppliers to take their business elsewhere if they do not like the division of duties and resources which has been implemented. The shareholders are not, in any interesting sense, the 'owners' of the company and the view of the functions of the corporation which sees it as the exercise of property rights is at best unhelpful.[4]

The successful management team in a business is one which strikes a balance with which most of these stakeholders are content, though rarely all at any particular time – maintaining a balance is the complex task of senior management. Investors are content with their dividend and share-price appreciation, employees happy with their jobs, customers and suppliers believe they are getting a good deal. So staff turnover is low, customers and suppliers remain loyal, and the shareholders do not sell their shares – which is overwhelmingly the normal response of investors and asset managers to dissatisfaction with management performance. That is how successful business actually operates.

A second feature of the account given by Blair and Stout is that while, as corporate lawyers, they are writing about business corporations, nothing in their description is in any way specific to a commercial enterprise. The concept of mediating hierarchy is relevant to almost any collective or community activity, private or public. There are some – schools and a few churches, and parts of the military – where acknowledgement of a strictly ordered hierarchy is intrinsic to the nature of the enterprise. But these are the exceptions rather than the norm. And to run a large business organization in this way, whether as an implementation of the far-seeing plans of 'the man who knows', or the pyramid of principal-agent incentive structures initiated by diverse shareholders, is simply impractical.

The mediating hierarchy is descriptive of how the faculty of most schools, almost all universities and the medical staff of a hospital are organized. Mediating hierarchy is necessary for them to be cohesive and effective. And a functioning sports club or charity will need to seek a similar structure. Thus the notion that there is, or needs to be, a sharp distinction between public and private business, between for-profit and not-for-profit enterprises, is largely illusory.

The more important distinction is between the authoritarian or contractual hierarchy, in which instructions cascade down, and the mediating hierarchy, in which roles and information are the subject of constant negotiation and whose members are free to leave if they are insufficiently satisfied with the functions they are being asked to perform. A business organization of any size and complexity is neces-sarily of this latter kind; it functions only as a voluntary community sustaining the consent of its members.

We suspect many readers nodded approvingly at the passage from Blair and Stout without recognizing its radicalism. That radicalism relates more to the way we *describe* business than to how it actu-ally operates. But we do not underestimate the importance of the description of business for its practice, and the importance of both description and practice for the legitimacy of commercial activity in the broader community.

THE CHANGE WE NEED

We frequently hear – even from senior executives – the claim that the managers of companies have a legal obligation to maximize profits or shareholder value. There is no such obligation, in Britain, or the

United States, or in any other major jurisdiction. In Britain, the duty of directors is 'to promote the success of the company for the benefit of the members'. This formulation is intentionally opaque, but the direction is clear: the benefit of the members is *the result* of the success of the company, not *the measure* of the success of the company. The management-friendly law of the state of Delaware, the principal jurisdiction for US corporations, is based on a business-judgement rule: except in a few specifically delineated situations, the court will uphold the honest exercise of managerial discretion.

Before the financialization of business and the economy more generally which began in the 1960s, salaried managers paid little attention to stockholders. The emphasis on shareholder interests in the past half-century is not the result of any change or clarification of corporate law, but a product of the era of market fundamentalism and 'greed is good'. That emphasis is the result of pressure from financial markets and financial interests, underpinned by the flimsy intellectual foundations provided by Friedman and others. It reflects the climate of the time, and if the climate changes in one direction, it can, and should, change in another.

At last there are signs that the weather is indeed becoming more benign. 'Purpose' is a new business buzzword, redolent of George Merck's 'we never forget that medicine is for the people, not the profits'. In August 2019, on the initiative of Alex Gorsky, the CEO of Johnson & Johnson, whose guiding, purpose-driven 'credo' we encountered in Chapter 2, America's Business Roundtable officially rescinded the guidance it had given since the 1990s. For thirty years it had reproduced the mantra that the purpose of a business was to maximize shareholder value. Acknowledging that this was not what many CEOs had actually been doing, it issued a new guide which enumerated five stakeholders: community, employees, customers, suppliers and shareholders, qualifying the last as a commitment only to 'long-term value'.[5] This stance would be approved by many of the world's largest shareholders, such as Norway's sovereign wealth fund (assets around $1 trillion) and the California Public Employees Retirement Scheme (assets around $400 billion), both of which have extensive concern with productive management engagement. Larry Fink, who leads BlackRock, the world's largest asset-management firm, writes an annual letter to his fellow CEOs. In 2018 he told them that business must have a purpose beyond profit.

In 2019, however, Fink's message had changed: corporations had a responsibility to intervene in matters which governments were failing to tackle effectively; and in 2020, in case that coded critique of President Trump's climate policy had been too obscure, his letter focussed explicitly on climate change. There are indeed some businesses, most obviously energy companies, for which climate change is a major issue. But the majority of companies are neither a material part of the climate problem nor a material part of the solution. We attend conferences which discuss ESG (environmental, social and governance) issues in business and investment at which business leaders and asset managers express their deep concern about climate change, their worries about 'inequality' (of what is rarely specified) and the need to have more BAME (black, Asian, minority ethnic) faces on boards and to reduce the 'gender pay gap'.

These are the issues which concern modern 'activists', few of whom have any real interest in business. The corporate leaders who deliver these speeches have discovered that these stirring sentiments win approbation from their audience while diverting attention from matters such as executive pay and corporate-tax avoidance. The social responsibility of the CEO is not to maximize their company's profits, but nor is it the 'activist' agenda: 'to intervene in matters in which governments were failing to tackle effectively'. It is to perform well the proper functions of business – to produce goods and services which customers want and value, to provide satisfying employment, to earn good returns for investors, to make a positive contribution to the communities in which they operate, and perhaps to set an example of moderation and modesty. Subject to the important caveat set out in Chapter 9, that businesses should not profit by creating problems for society, these proper functions *are* the business of business. Mr Fink is doing a great job in almost all of them. But in the midst of the economic meltdown from COVID-19, he has just accepted a 5 per cent pay increase – raising his salary to $25 million.

INDUSTRIAL DEMOCRACY

Legitimate business works for all its stakeholders – customers, employees, investors and communities. But that does not require a form of industrial democracy in which companies are governed by a board comprising representatives of all these stakeholder groups. Advocates of this kind of participatory democracy in business are making the same mistake as advocates of this kind of participatory democracy in politics. The mistake fuses the triumph of greed – I acknowledge the validity of no interest other than my own – with the culture of rights – I declare my interest by strident insistence on it – and the politics of identity – a group interest can only be validly understood by a member of that group.

The people who work in Airbus factories, or the passengers who fly in their planes, have little more insight into what the next generation of Airbus products should be than anyone else. No doubt many of them could acquire such insight – by the extended study of competing products, the needs of airlines and the technical characteristics of engines and flight-control systems. But to do so would be a full-time occupation, and then the individuals concerned would no longer sensibly be employed as designers of aircraft wings or speakers at international conferences. They would have become qualified professional managers of an aircraft-manufacturing business. In business, as in politics, we require the services of honest men and women trying to do the best for their community, large or small, not selfish individuals pursuing their own best interests. And certainly not professional representatives furthering their own best interests by advocating the best interests of the group which has appointed or hired them.

Nor do we favour reforms which would give workers rights to shares in the company. Rewarding employees of start-ups with options or shares, rather than cash, which the fledgeling business may not have, is a sensible way of financing such businesses, and necessarily strengthens the beneficiaries' identification with the company. And if it is necessary or desirable to pay senior executives bonuses – which we doubt – then doing so in blocked shares may help ensure that their interest in the prosperity of the company extends beyond their own tenure. But committed employees already have a large investment in the business for which they work – and, unlike shareholders, one they cannot sell. The example of Enron, where workers taken in by the hype lost not only their jobs but their savings, is salutary. The purpose of firms should be reset not by committing workers through channelling their savings into shareholdings, but by recognizing their existing commitment and understanding that employees 'own' the company every bit as much as shareholders.

THE MARKET AND THE COMMUNITY

In Chapter 8 we referred to various modern communitarian philosophers such as Etzioni and MacIntyre, Sandel and Walzer. One thing these writers have in common, regardless of their manifold differences, is a fear that community is being eroded by the practices of the market and the values, or lack of them, of modern business. Walzer's best-known work is *Spheres of Justice*, which declares a need to ringfence the moral and political world from the influence of economics. Sandel's widely acclaimed *What Money Can't Buy: The Moral Limits of Markets* attempts to identify those areas of life which must be kept free from market forces. Macpherson coined the term 'possessive individualism' and wrote an extended essay critical of the moral philosophy implicit in the work of Milton Friedman. And of course Aristotle, while admiring of productive activity, had despised the middle man. It would have been hard for him to imagine trade in securitized financial products, but it is not hard to imagine what he would have thought about it if he had.

For ideas to matter, they must find practical application. The communitarian philosophers cannot be blamed for dismissing modern economics: the economics of individualism is indeed repellent. But in supposing an intrinsic tension between the community and the economy, they marginalized the ideas in which they believe. The notion that community and market are antithetical is a recent one. Historically, the opposite was true.

The agora in ancient Greece and the forum in ancient Rome were both marketplaces and meeting places. In classical Greek, the words for 'to shop' and 'to speak in public' are similar, derivations of the same root. And when one of us recently asked a taxi driver to take us to the centre of the small capital of his poor country, he deposited us in a busy location and pointed. 'There is the old market, straight ahead,' he said, and 'There is the new market, to the right.' For most of history, and in less-developed countries today, the marketplace was not the enemy of community: the marketplace was where community came to life. Indeed, the market is the process that replaces the isolation of self-sufficiency with the communalism of interdependence. The institution of the market is the essential first step in the journey out of mass poverty.

And even today if you ask a taxi driver to take you to the centre of an English town, he will drive you to the high street and you will see the familiar branches of Boots, W. H. Smith and Starbucks. You will find a plethora of commentary on the role of the hollowing-out of the high street and its unfortunate impact on the community.

When Adam Smith wrote that 'It is not from the benevolence of the butcher, the brewer, or the baker that we expect our dinner, but from their regard to their own interest,' he was not describing Amalgamated Meats plc, United Beers Ltd or the International Bread Corporation (and certainly not the National Bread Service).[6] He was describing the artisan who ran a local shop and knew most of his customers, with whom he enjoyed a personal relationship. 'The mutton is very good today, Mrs Smith,' the butcher would advise.

Only in the following century, as economies of scale and the ambitions of tycoons and financiers established the large corporations which came to dominate twentieth-century business, did anonymous transactions generally displace exchanges which were embedded in continuing relationships. It was, and is, that change which justified the concern that markets and community were antithetical.

But from the beginnings of modern business, it was realized that consumers would be reluctant to trade anonymously. When the local shop began to trade in industrially manufactured products, the makers of these products began to engage in branding and advertising; by spending money promoting the product, they sought to demonstrate their permanence and establish a continuing relationship. And as goods became more complex, anonymity became harder and harder to maintain. Very few of the exchanges we make as consumers in a modern economy, and almost none of the commercial exchanges, are trades between anonymous buyers and anonymous sellers of homogeneous products. Many devices have emerged to replace the advice and gossip in the butcher's shop, but even among large multinational corporations personal relationships continue to matter; the business-class cabins of aircraft are filled with executives for whom video conferencing is still inferior to a handshake and a shared meal. (As we write, during the coronavirus crisis, these cabins are empty – we will learn how quickly the cabins refill and the Zoom screens go blank when the crisis is over.)

The internet and other aspects of globalization have made it possible for every potential seller to contact every potential buyer, and vice versa. But at the same time devices have emerged to make it possible to trade confidently with someone we do not know. Airbnb and Uber enable us to stay safely in a stranger's home and ride safely in a stranger's car. And they deliver a profile of Bill the host or Rashid the driver. The community of Amazon bookbuyers rates every book on its site, eBay users rank its sellers, and TripAdvisor assembles opinions on hotels, restaurants and attractions. While the butcher learned of the preferences of Mrs Smith, and Adam from her regular shopping patterns, so the supermarket derives the same information from your loyalty card. And just as the butcher would have made recommendations to Mrs Smith derived from his understanding of these preferences, Google and Amazon anticipate the new products we might want to buy. What customers fear is not that online sellers and Google and Facebook know too little about us, but that they know too much.

The need for community is fundamental to both social and economic life, and as technology and social change have diminished the effectiveness of some forms of community, they have simultaneously and necessarily increased the opportunities for others. Markets are not intrinsically inimical to community; indeed, effective markets today are, as they always have been, embedded in communities.

The first decade of the present century offered a forceful demonstration of this enduring truth. Lending transactions were traditionally based on personal relationships. J. P. Morgan, no enemy of market fundamentalism, observed that the basis of lending was character and that 'A man I do not trust could not get money from me on all the bonds in Christendom.'[7] A bank loan required a grilling from an unsympathetic branch manager, who got to know his business customers and many of his personal ones through the golf club; a mortgage was grudgingly offered to customers who had built up savings and necessitated a visit to the building-society office. In the 1980s this community-based approach was largely replaced by automated credit-scoring of loans and their resale in packages through securitization. The 2008 global financial crisis was the direct result.

12

Communities of Place

'The ache for home lives in all of us.'
— Maya Angelou, *All God's Children*
Need Traveling Shoes

When constructive activists wanted to get Londoners to work together for a common purpose they named the new organization Little Village. Of course, London, with its anomie and extremes of wealth and poverty, is the antithesis of a village, but in that poignant aspiration they were tapping into a deep instinct: *Homo sapiens*, like many species, bonds to place.

Place matters both psychologically and politically. The power of decision should be increasingly decentralized, and the most important single dimension of that decentralization is spatial. Place is a fundamental identity that takes us beyond ourselves and beyond the present, connecting us with an enduring community. Many aspects of personal identity are forged in our early teens, and remember: most British people still live within twenty miles of where they were when fourteen. Even in an age of social media, physical proximity enables a higher quality of human interaction: the mutual trust which is essential for much of modernity is often built through the tacit knowledge of another person that can only come from repeated face-to-face meetings. The randomness of spatial encounters so eloquently described by Jane Jacobs in her description of life in the streets of Manhattan offers us more diversity of opinion than the echo-chambers of social media.[1] Vibrant communities-of-place are the social analogue of the economy of thriving small businesses – the 'little platoons' from whose competition and cooperation an innovative yet cohesive society can be formed. Britain's imposing Victorian town halls are testimony to an era when we had many such little platoons around the country. Yet they stand today as symbols of a municipal self-confidence that has all but vanished.

HYPER-CENTRALIZATION

It is not only government which is centralized in London. Britain's media, business, law and finance are all based there. And each of these activities has itself become more centralized. Finance always starts as localized, because lending decisions depend on the tacit knowledge that can only come from long local presence: guess where the Midland Bank started. Concentration in banking was supported as a means of reducing risks to depositors and shareholders, a strategy which worked for a hundred years, until the early years of the twenty-first century, when it turned out to have concentrated folly.

The tight control over local-government finances exercised by the Treasury is more recent, dating from the 1980s. The effects of insistence on Treasury control are found everywhere. Attempts to decentralize – whether to devolved governments, academies running schools or NHS trusts running hospitals – are all constrained by the requirement that overall financial control remains with Whitehall. But responsibility and financial autonomy are inseparable, as every parent learns. Whatever the nature of British failure – in providing local-government services, maintaining standards in education in the devolved nations, or raising hospital effectiveness – the fault is attributed to government unwillingness to provide enough money. Sometimes the claim is justified, sometimes not. But there is no need even to think about that question, or engage in self-examination, because blame always lies somewhere else. And the process is self-reinforcing and self-justifying: agencies which are not given financial autonomy do not acquire the capacity to exercise it responsibly.

Centralization has coincided with divergence: by 2018, output per person was £54,700 in London versus £23,600 in the north-east.[2] Divergence continues. The capital region now accounts for 23 per cent of national output, up from 18 per cent in 1998.[3] Some market fundamentalists believe that such extreme agglomeration is allocatively efficient: people in London are highly productive, especially the skilled, and so concentrating more skilled people in London is even more efficient. If we must worry about spatial fairness, they would argue, the best approach is to transfer consumption to provincial towns and cities through taxes and benefits,* just as we can stabilize meritocracy by raising taxes from the meritocrats to fund benefits for the left-behind.

But we are not just consumers. Most people want the dignity that comes from being able to contribute to their community and their society. They want to be productive. What needs to be spread more equally around the country is the capacity to be productive, not just the capacity to consume. The phrase 'the capacity to be productive' combines two related but distinct processes: productive jobs need to come to the places where people belong, and young people in those places need to be equipped to do them. Skilled jobs without locally equipped people lead firms to bring in skilled non-locals, deepening the alienation and demoralization of the local population. Conversely, training people for whom there are no local jobs simply reinforces pressures on the ablest young people to leave.

Extreme concentrations of people in megacities result in a loss of liveability. Although London is efficient at transforming effort into income, it is inefficient at transforming income into well-being. London is the region with the highest average income in the UK, but the region with the *lowest* average score on 'well-being'.[†] To be rich or young in London can be highly agreeable; only a few other megacities offer culture and clubbing of comparable quality. But only the rich can afford flats and houses in central London and only the young can tolerate living in bedsits. The material conditions of

* See, for example, the dismissive description of provincial Britain as viewed from London, advanced in the *Financial Times* by Janan Ganesh, as like being 'shackled to a corpse', or the similarly dismissive term 'fly-over cities' used in the United States.
† Office for National Statistics (23 Oct. 2019). 'Well-being' is defined by the ONS as being composed of Life Satisfaction (London scores lowest), Worthwhile (London scores lowest), Happiness (London scores second lowest, with a score of 7.51; Yorkshire and Humber are lowest, with a score of 7.49) and Anxiety (London scores highest).

congestion reflected in crowded commuting and lack of floor space, and the social isolation reflected in a loss of proximity to family and belonging to community, are likely explanations of the gap between income and well-being.

And if we look outside Britain, we see that productivity can be well distributed spatially while overall being very high: 'come to London' is unnecessary. Germany has Hamburg in the north-west, Berlin in the north-east, Frankfurt and Cologne in the west, Stuttgart in the centre, and Munich in the south-east: all prosperous and confident cities.

A Britain in which prosperity was widely distributed around the country would be a better society. To reverse hyper-centralization, the power of decision in government and business needs to be devolved from London to the regions, cities and towns. But spatial equilibria are analogous to social equilibria: a good spatial equilibrium is fairly robust, but so is hyper-concentration. Getting the dinghy righted is no small matter.

Eastern Germany since 1990 illustrates the problem of a dinghy which had capsized. After two decades of active policy and massive fiscal transfers, although the former East Germany has achieved considerable convergence of consumption, it has yet to achieve a convergence of productive work and dignity. The attempt to create a single country is widely seen as a failure, manifest in the emergence of grievance over 'second-class citizenship' and the support for extremist parties.

In Britain, the most successful city outside London is Edinburgh. The comparison of Edinburgh with the successful dispersion of knowledge-clusters in western Germany and limited successes in eastern Germany may help to explain what is needed for successful convergence. The capacity to be productive involves both bringing productive jobs to the places where people belong and equipping local people with the skills to do them.

BRINGING PRODUCTIVE JOBS TO THE PLACES WHERE PEOPLE BELONG

Jobs are not brought to places by fast railways. Edinburgh and the cities of western Germany have succeeded through a combination of many factors: financial, industrial, cultural, educational. Broken towns and cities often lack all of these elements and, unless this is understood, piecemeal attempts at change are doomed to fail, deepening demoralization. These cities are locked in a syndrome in which, because everything depends upon everything else, changing any one characteristic, although in fact necessary, fails to deliver significant improvements and so appears to be useless. The real message is not 'do nothing,' but 'do everything' by following an informed, forward-looking common purpose. A leader cannot save a broken city single-handed: the communitarian leader's job is to harness the potential of many local organizations.

For this to happen, political autonomy at the appropriate levels is an essential characteristic: towns, cities and regions each need authority for actions best coordinated at that level. In Germany, this is an implication of the federal constitution: the city within its region. For a high-productivity modern economy, this looks to be the right level at which to concentrate policy decisions. Britain is belatedly creating them: the new city-region combined authorities, such as the one created in the West Midlands, created in 2017 with a population of 3 million. Initially, the city-regions were not particularly popular: in reaction to the strident nationalism of Scotland, many English people wanted a rival political body. But political authority needs to be set at a level appropriate for a modern economy, and for that England is too big – essentially, it would perpetuate rule from Whitehall. Conversely, the forty-eight counties of England are mostly too small: city-regions are the level which makes economic sense. Regional identities might not prove difficult to revive: Anglo-Saxon entities such as Mercia provide ample depth of history on which to craft new narratives of identity. Not just power but identities can adjust to circumstances. Scotland is both a political identity and a natural region and so many functions of government were being exercised from Edinburgh long before Scotland achieved its own legislature and government in 1999.

Locally based finance has an overarching alignment of long-term purpose regarding local prosperity and the tacit knowledge in lending decisions that comes from frequent personal contact with the management of local firms. Most banking for German industry is still undertaken by regional institutions. Scottish banks were not consolidated into London-based pan-British banks until the financial crisis of 2008, and still retain substantial headquarters operations in Edinburgh. In contrast, Wales, although having a similar degree of political devolution, has no local finance industry. Even in Cardiff, the capital, the branches of the London-headquartered banks no longer retain account managers. The tacit knowledge of local experience has been lost.

Business communities tend to organize themselves so as to be able to lobby near to political and financial decision-taking. In Edinburgh and most German cities, business organizations are local, while in England they are national, and clustered in London. In Germany, public policy has considerably encouraged local business organizations by legislation which gives them important functions.

Former US Senator Moynihan reportedly said 'to create a great city, create a great university and wait 200 years', and there are many examples around the world to make his point. Their potential importance to the local economy is partly for training in locally pertinent skills, and partly to generate research that helps to keep knowledge-intensive firms sufficiently close to the frontier that they can sustain their position. Again, public policy can help or impede links between education and local business. For example, in the 1980s Britain converted its locally oriented technical colleges – 'polytechnics' – into universities, and this changed their sources of finance, reducing their links to local government and local business. German tertiary education has far stronger links with local business, through its prestigious vocational training programmes.

The presence of a university contributes to a strong sense of local culture, one which attracts talented people who are not necessarily associated with the university. We can testify to the strength of this effect from our knowledge of Oxford house prices. Civic society in Edinburgh pioneered the city's annual festival, which has created a 'brand' attracting 500,000 people from around the world. German cities have particularly strong civic society, partly because public policy encourages participation in *Vereine* (associations). If de Tocqueville had been alive today, he might have been writing about the German propensity to join *Vereine*.

Devolved public finance empowers local political leadership to upgrade the infrastructure that can anchor a new narrative and which can be used to encourage the other local actors to collaborate. The threat of Scottish nationalism has sustained a large fiscal transfer to the Edinburgh-based Scottish government. Public spending in Scotland has been approximately 15 per cent higher than that in England.[4]

Good local leadership forges purposive collaboration between local government, local business, local colleges and local civic society. The purpose must be well informed, forward-looking and seen as mutually beneficial so it can be held in common. In Edinburgh in 2009, leaders brought the various local entities together to agree on attracting a sector that had the potential to generate knowledge-intensive jobs: they chose information technology. At the time, the city had only two such firms, but with each entity playing its role, Edinburgh was able to attract many more. As of 2019, Edinburgh had 480 IT firms – the largest cluster in Europe.* Again, public policy can help or hinder the emergence of good local leadership. Germany has long had powerful mayors. Being a clear route to the top of national politics, these positions attract highly able people: for example, Germany's current Minister of Finance and Deputy Chancellor was previously the Mayor of Hamburg. In contrast, England is only now piloting the idea of directly elected mayors.

Not only can these characteristics account for the success of Edinburgh and the cities of western Germany, but their absence from other UK cities may also help to explain both why Britain has greater spatial inequality than Germany, and why, although East Germany has caught up with the West in terms of consumption, its population has become disaffected.

On German reunification in 1990, the East did not start with local business communities (or local anything): its communist state

---

* Paul thanks the fifteen staff of Edinburgh University's Business School and the Edinburgh Futures Institute who hosted him and his colleague Professor Mayer at a dinner following their British Academy Lecture on the role of business and public policy in healing social divergence. Their collective briefing on the city's strategy was invaluable.

enterprises were nationally organized. The massive financial transfers from West to East which followed had as their prime purpose to raise per capita consumption and to attract subsidiary operations of West German businesses rather than to build prosperous local businesses. Hence, East Germany has been slow to develop locally rooted business communities. Further, the GDR police state had undermined local social cohesion and cooperation: for good reason, people had become distrustful of each other and had little experience of local collective initiative. East Germany was run centrally from Berlin. The national policies implemented in post-1990 East Germany have consequently not enabled most of its cities to build the interdependent clusters of knowledge-intensive firms which would have retained bright young people. Instead, its cities have filled up with low-cost, low-skill enterprises. While consumption levels have risen, productivity has stalled significantly below West German levels.[5]

Cities with none of these characteristics are trapped, but escape is made all the harder because the main means by which humans learn a skill is by doing it. In a successful city, the meta-skill that has been learned by doing is the capacity to devise a viable forward-looking strategy and cohere around it. Broken cities do not have this capacity to draw upon. Steeped in failure, the entities in a broken city each seek an explanation for that failure, and discover that they are victims. There are always candidate oppressors: the metropolis – 'We're poor because London's rich' – or some other local entity – 'This place is hopeless for business because the council is hostile to enterprise.' These narratives of grievance may well have some basis in fact, but this does not stop them being incapacitating. Far from being informed, forward-looking, of common purpose, they are self-justifying, backward-looking and oppositional. They incite futile struggles that divert energy from what needs to happen. That is why broken cities need good leadership. Only trusted local leaders can reset the narrative from backward-looking grievance to forward-looking common purpose. Scotland congratulates itself on success; Wales blames England for its failures – the leader of the Welsh Nationalists is currently demanding 'reparations' for English economic oppression.[6]

EQUIPPING LOCAL PEOPLE TO DO
THE PRODUCTIVE LOCAL JOBS

Skill accumulation must necessarily occur through two distinct paths. Universities deepen the abilities of those young adults well suited to cognitively focussed education, and this provides a cognitive platform on which specialist professional skills can be built. This process is generally working well in Britain. But young adults whose abilities are less suited to cognitively focussed education need to make a more demanding transition to the acquisition of a range of non-cognitive, vocational skills. This process varies considerably around Europe, with Britain being among the least successful at it.

Fortunately, the diverse range of policies important for non-cognitive-skill accumulation around Europe provides a natural arena for rapid social learning and imitation. The process which results in a young adult who is fully equipped with the necessary practical skills to be productive, and then maintains them, consists of a long chain of distinct phases, each dependent upon specific supportive public policies. At present, in Britain's broken cities, poor families are often wary of encouraging their children into their full skill potential, fearing that, since there are no skilled local jobs, if they become skilled they will leave. Thus, encouraging young people to get training and encouraging firms to bring in productive jobs are interdependent. The answer is not 'do neither' but 'do both'.

Delivering good vocational training may need to begin early in life. A poor family stressed by an unmanageable toddler will find it hard to give adequate attention to keeping a teenager with ADHD on track in schooling. Effective support for the toddler might free up mental bandwidth for managing the teenager; although no country has a complete chain of such policies that are best practice, for each phase there is at least one that is successful.

Capacities are forged from conception. The 9/11 terrorist attacks on the World Trade Center imposed stress on pregnant women in New York and studies have found adverse epigenetic consequences for their babies.[7] Once started, disadvantage continues: 'maternal stress in the first year is especially disruptive of infant-mother attachment and caregiving.'[8] And such disadvantage may persist; when causes are interdependent, as in epigenetics, certainty may be beyond reach: public policy must act on judgement and precaution. Given that the circumstances that typically trigger stress in pregnancy are easy to spot, and preventive remedies less costly than coping with the damage, the implication is clear. More generally, during the period from conception to the age of around three years, the priority seems to be to support young mothers and strengthen their families. An example of such practical support in the home is the Dutch policy of providing home-helpers to mothers facing demanding situations: Mary Poppins targeted not in the homes of the affluent, where nannies are currently concentrated, but where they are of most value.

In contrast, the British social-work system is designed around scrutiny of parents under threat of child-removal: currently, 80,000 children are being reared in foster care.[9] Some foster carers are wonderful, but foster care is temporary and it is paid; children thrive when they know that they are in a secure, well-motivated environment of unconditional love. Meanwhile, the scrutiny role of social workers, built around the mantra that 'safeguarding of the child is the top priority', virtually condemns the relationship between the worker and the family to failure. In 2002, the chief executive of the General Social Care Council described what has happened to the system: 'The thing is that nowadays you're not really responsible to a person, you're responsible to a rule book.'[10] Decision-by-rulebook intentionally eliminates judgement based on tacit knowledge. Hilary Cottam estimates that more than 80 per cent of the typical social worker's time is now taken merely administering the intricate system of scrutiny necessary to absolve social-work departments for any liability for the inevitable failures.[11] As with the health service, the tasks are so complex that, even with a well-resourced and decentralized decision-taking structure, things would sometimes go wrong. The attempt to *deflect* responsibility from such failures, rather than *address* them, dooms the system to far worse outcomes. Workers who have the tacit knowledge of family context are denied freedom of judgement: they must follow the protocol of 'safeguarding'; they must 'remove on suspicion'. The work is so demoralizing that turnover is high, further undermining tacit knowledge. The structure of scrutiny is complex and fragmented.

Council budgets for social work are exhausted by this vast edifice of scrutiny of families and monitoring of staff. But even the balance of a social worker's time that is not exhausted by administration – the time that is spent with the problem family – is misused. The priority of the social worker is to gather the data that is needed for the system of scrutiny. Meanwhile, the family, knowing that it is being scrutinized with the threat of child-removal, cannot afford to trust the person who is ostensibly there to help them. The priority for the family is concealment. The mother perceives herself under siege. As Cottam recounts, a stressed mother juggling tasks will commonly have two phones: one for the small group she trusts – often people in the same position – and the other to 'manage the social'.[12] She will be fending off the danger that her children will be removed, while trying to access benefits. Hence, British social work is a microcosm of the failures of organizations that try to achieve a highly complex task through a highly centralized structure of monitoring and penalties. It doesn't work anywhere, and it doesn't work here.

Between the ages of two and five, a child's capacities can be enhanced by socialization. A good model is the French pre-school system of *écoles maternelles*. One strength of this system is that it is free, and standardized, so that attendance has become the social norm. Hence, there is no stigma attached to it, so that the children who are most in need of it are very likely to be sent by their parents. Because provision is by means of formal entities, with a headmistress and professionally qualified staff, children get a structured learning experience within which their progress can be monitored. Additionally, being a fully-fledged organization, it can readily catalyse a community among parents, reducing the stress of isolation. Standards and finance for pre-school education exemplify a task that is sufficiently straightforward for government, most likely at local level, to do well, with management further decentralized to include civil society organizations such as churches.

By the age of six, the cognitive performance of the future eighteen-year-old is largely set.[13] While the years of schooling receive enormous policy attention, Robert Putnam argues convincingly that schools are predominantly *sites* in which children interact, and thereby influence each other, as well as *organizations* that feed them information. Since the social composition of catchment areas differs according to house prices, schools in high-price areas thereby amplify the cultural advantages with which well-educated parents individually endow their children, and so reinforce rather than mitigate earlier differences.[14] Assortative mating, followed by assortative location, leaves schools little scope for redressing weaknesses. Again, an implication is that resources should be focussed on the first six years. There are, however, substantial variations around Europe in school practices, with Finland recognized as having among the most successful outcomes.

Post-school, there are wide variations in the provision of vocational training. One unsurprising lesson from failures in vocational training is that local firms need to be fully involved in its design and execution.[15] Another is that to achieve a high level of skill, and the ability to acquire related skills, courses need to be long – typically three to four years – and properly accredited. A particularly successful model is that in Switzerland, where 60 per cent of school-leavers choose to take the vocational route.[16] Firms have a strong incentive to be involved with the course because they finance half of the costs. Britain's training colleges are severely underfunded and often not well integrated into local business; there may not even be a local business association with which the colleges could liaise. There are too many different types of course (over 700 versus around 200 in Germany), too narrowly focussed, too short – often just a few months versus three years elsewhere. And there is no obvious progression from one to another and then on to a productive job. In contrast to university, there is no clear trajectory that a young person can use to chart a future. Indeed, further education is so confusingly fragmented that not even their mentors can advise students.

THE IMPLICATION

Place matters: Brexit, and its bitter divisions, is part of the price that Britain has paid for neglecting that evident fact. *Recreating* towns and cities that consist of a proud mosaic of organizations – firms, families, public services and civil society – through which they equip their people with the capacity to be productive, is challenging. But, once recreated, vibrant places are largely self-sustaining. *Homo sapiens*, as distinct from Economic Man, finds it natural to work together for a forward-looking common purpose, and to do so through bonding to place. *Neighbourliness is natural.*

Titus Salt, that local businessman-turned-mayor in the Bradford of the 1840s, built trust through self-sacrificing practical actions, giving his fortune away to his workforce and city. In contrast, Mrs Jellyby's effusive and narcissistic emoting for a place that she has never seen is mere artifice. Salt was an example of how leadership catalysed common, forward-looking purpose: his statue, erected by a grateful population, stands in testimony. He was a pioneer of business-in-the-community. Will our business schools produce a George Merck, who thought that medicine was for the people and built a great company, or a Michael Pearson, who thought medicine was for the profits and destroyed a smaller one? Will Davos celebrate the activism of Sir Titus or throw its arms round Mrs Jellyby?

Epilogue: Shelter from the Storm

'We expect too much of new buildings, and too little of our-selves'

– Jane Jacobs, *The Death and Life of Great American Cities,* 1961

POLITICS

Like other successful societies, Britain has a political system which worked reasonably well for a century, its two parties mostly finding competent leaders, alternating them in office and encouraging them to move towards a moderate consensus. We have described how this cohesive centrism, which had survived two wars and a great depression, fell apart. As it did, one party was focussed on a statist ideology which failed. The other was a coalition which fell apart, briefly captured by a market fundamentalist ideology, now also discredited, and then obsessed with the issue of British membership of the European Union. Today, the membership of each has shrunk to a rump of people who are highly unrepresentative of our society, one in which activists and extremists are prominent. Fortunately, Britain now has an opportunity: both main parties have pragmatic new leaders with the power to reset their party's agendas.

We seek a restoration of representative government based on parties which are themselves broad coalitions of loosely like-minded people. These parties need to become more representative of their supporters and potential supporters. Participation is not democratic when those who participate are themselves unrepresentative. There should be many routes into national politics, as there once were – the stepping stones of local government, unions and other community organizations.

And that requires us to revive these organizations, to experiment with the German model of public funding for *Vereine* – registered clubs and associations. Money helps associations form and sustain themselves: whereas in Britain social isolation is increasing, in Germany the membership of *Vereine* has increased by around a third, and almost half the population are members.[1] Loneliness is now the main disease in Britain. We don't need WeWork, but we do need WePlay.

BUSINESS

And yet the absurd Neumann was on to something. Businesses are the most important communities we have. CEOs are now falling over themselves to announce that they want their firm to be prosocial. But this must not be a matter of greenwash. We told the story of the pharmaceutical industry at some length because it illustrates so clearly what socially responsible business really means – the provision of life-improving goods and services to the community in ways that offer satisfying employment while being financially self-sustaining. And the same industry illustrates what socially responsible business should *not* mean – maximizing profits by corrupting professionals and exploiting the vulnerable. We could have given a similar account of what has happened in financial services and several other industries. The social responsibility of business is to conduct business in a socially responsible way.

This is a matter of culture rather than law – existing law certainly permits and arguably requires such behaviour. If there is a case for new corporate legislation, that case is mainly that such debate would focus attention on the role of business in society in a way which would end the current corrosive rhetoric and dysfunctional bonus culture of market fundamentalism. And perhaps mitigate the too often malign influence of the modern finance sector on non-financial business.

CARE

The thoughtful Labour MP Liz Kendall has pondered what can be done to improve care for the elderly in England, a vital subject which successive governments have found too difficult to tackle. She poses the problem as 'What is the right balance between the contributions made by individuals and the state?' And her solution is 'a joined-up service' between the NHS and social care, with 'a single budget' and 'a single commissioning body'.[2] Her very characterization of the question insists on the dichotomy of individual-versus-state. And her solution reveals that persistent instinct to over-centralization. She is proposing to merge two vast organizations, each with tasks too complex to be managed, into an even larger organization to undertake a task more complex still. Who, navigating from 'common sense', could oppose the idea that services should be 'joined up'? Well, people like us. We have studied the evidence of failure and seen the value of the pluralism and flexibility of multiple initiatives. Who is in charge of the supply of bread to New York?

It is hard to think of an activity better suited to small, localized initiatives than care of the elderly. Community organizations can flexibly combine part-time volunteers with skilled professionals and helpful neighbours. They can build links within the community sensitive to changing local needs. They can listen to old people themselves – not to activists and lobbyists making representations on their behalf, as central organizations do and must – but to individuals. When Hilary Cottam encountered an old man who was desperately lonely, she took the time to understand from him what would make his life brighter. The result was ridiculously simple: through a little organizational effort, he and others were routinely reconnected by phone with the music they had loved and the people they had known. There is an astonishing capacity within every community for such initiatives, and there are already many thousands of them.

DECENTRALIZING GOVERNMENT

Treasury control has removed much financial autonomy from local authorities. We have introduced measures of decentralization in activities such as health and education, but severely limited their authority and their acquisition of skills by denying them real financial autonomy. The centralized state has attempted to devolve responsibility for failure, rather than the means for achieving success. And so decentralization is a sham unless accompanied by a capacity to determine revenue and expenditure. As the governments of regions, cities and towns gain real power, aspiring politicians will join them and the most successful will become nationally prominent. Devolved power will gradually help to solve the need for a more representative politics.

A shift in public spending from London to the North is long overdue, and will need to be sustained for decades to rectify past imbalances. But this should not be a revival of the New Labour agenda of transferring consumption from the booming metropolis. The regions need clusters of productive jobs and their people need the training through which they are equipped to do them. It is the productivity gap, not merely the consumption gap, that needs to be closed. These tasks are not easy: they call for a massive and sustained effort, funded nationally but run locally. London is disproportionate not only in public spending but in its media influence. The views of London's people matter, perhaps more than they ought. Londoners can either launch themselves into the motivated reasoning of justifying self-interest or contribute to the reunification of the country by acknowledging the need to put things right.

THE STORM

Ideas usually take time to filter through, but with brutal speed, the crisis of coronavirus may have brought forward the moment at which community reasserts itself. Neither states nor individuals can shelter us from such a virus. Democratic states have built only modest powers of enforcement: we are citizens, not subjects. Individuals cannot self-isolate for life: the ugly counterpart of 'stand on your own feet' is 'fall on your own face'. Our vital resource is community. As we send this book to press, it is unclear whether our societies will find within them a sufficient sense of community to cooperate for this common good. But on the first day of the government's appeal for helpers, over half a million people volunteered.[3] The pandemic has demanded something of all of us: our best hope is that willing compliance is widespread. As always, only if the antisocial are a minority will the limited enforcement resources of the state be able to cope. If not, we may collapse into the consequences of self-serving individualism, as infected people continue to spread the virus and opportunists profit from the mounting disorder.

Pericles' funeral oration in 430BC, with which we began this book, celebrated Athens, the world's first civic community. Then the city was struck by a plague from which he died the following year. Thucydides reports that 'It was to the plague that Athens owed its unprecedented collapse into lawlessness.'[4] In Sparta, intense repression kept the plague at bay. But Athens never recovered and was defeated in the continuing Peloponnesian wars. The parallels are obvious, and disturbing. Western Europe has so far been successful not only in maintaining but in enhancing social cohesion. Soon, we will either be celebrating the value of community or contemplating the awful consequences of its loss.

FROM 'ME' TO 'WE' AND FROM US TO YOU

We are pragmatic economists, not romantic evangelists. Like all economists, we were taught that the world was populated by rational maximizing individuals, and we passed on this doctrine to our own students. But Paul's experience in African economies brought home to him that societies of selfish agents independently pursuing their own interests, in which all relationships outside the family or tribe were purely transactional, were not only among the poorest on the planet, but fated to remain so without social transformation. John learned that a model of business in which all relationships were transactional had nothing to do with how successful corporations actually worked, and that the financial crisis of 2008 demonstrated the predictable failure of firms structured around this belief. Successful corporations built groups of cooperating individuals, drew on collective knowledge and benefited from the intrinsic motivation which most people have to work together for a worthwhile purpose.

The state cannot and should not be the repository of all obligations, charged with securing a panoply of economic rights, and with missions of global salvationism or the growth of GDP. Subsidiarity assigns most obligations to much lower-level organizations; and the state is the servant of its citizens as expressed through participatory democracy. The intellectual tide is turning away from the adversarial tensions of individual-or-state. It will be superseded by a characterization of society as a myriad of small organizations, within each of which people find common purpose, and which collaborate in larger groupings for those common purposes that need scale.

Individualism is loneliness, not liberation; the shelter of the bunker ultimately fails. Belonging does not shackle us to burdens, it brings us home to our humanity. We hope that our short book has given you the confidence to join in.

Notes

PREFACE: WHY NOW?

1 https://www.moreincommon.com/media/bfwlsrxu/more-in
-common-the-new-normal-comparative-7-country-en.pdf.
2 https://www.pewresearch.org/2021/03/05/a-year-of-u-s-public
-opinion-on-the-coronavirus-pandemic/.
3 https://extinctionrebellion.uk/2020/04/15/we-were-the-boat-the
-inside-story-of-an-april-icon/.
4 https://www.gov.uk/government/speeches/home-secretary-speech
-at-the-police-superintendents-association-conference.
5 Tom Devine, *Scottish Review*, 3 February 2021.

1: WHAT IS GOING ON HERE?

1 J. F. Kennedy (20 Jan. 1961).
2 R. M. Nixon (20 Jan. 1973).
3 *Wall Street Journal* (19 July 2012).
4 R. Limbaugh (24 July 2012).
5 B. H. Obama (13 July 2012).
6 I. Boesky quoted in B. Greene (15 Dec. 1986).
7 J. Bentham, *The Book of Fallacies, Part V, Anarchical Fallacies*
(1843).
8 Goldman Sachs (2020) p. 1.
9 The We Company S-1 Form (2019).
10 E. Platt (5 Sept. 2019).
11 E. Platt (24 Dec. 2019).

2: INDIVIDUALIST ECONOMICS

1 In *An Extraordinary Time* (2016) Marc Levinson provides a good retrospective critique of Keynesian demand management.

2 G. Becker (1976), p. 14.

3 J. Waldfogel (2009).

4 The Committee for the Prize in Economic Sciences in Memory of Alfred Nobel (1992).

5 Quoted in C. Warren (1999), pp. 370–71.

6 J. Rousseau (1761), p. 105.

7 M. Friedman (13 Sept. 1970).

8 G. W. Merck (1 Dec. 1950).

9 *Fortune* (2020).

10 D. Crow (17 Nov. 2016).

11 D. Kozarich (27 Sept. 2016).

12 J. Hoffman (26 Aug. 2019).

13 H. Kuchler et al. (23 Jan. 2020).

14 Quoted in A. Chakrabortty (10 Jan. 2017).

15 C. Goodhart in D. E. Altig and B. D. Smith (2003), p. 67 fn. 1.

16 J. Bentham, J. H. Burns and H. L. A. Hart (1977), p. 393.

17 K. J. Arrow (1950).

18 P. Singer (1972), pp. 231–2.

19 G. Sidgwick (1962), p. 414.

20 F. P. Ramsey (1928). p. 543.

21 D. Goodhart (2017), p. 15.

22 M. Friedman and L. J. Savage (1948); K. J. Arrow and G. Debreu (1954).

23 M. C. Jensen and W. H. Meckling (1976); F. H. Easterbrook and D. R. Fischel (1996).

24 T. J. Sargent, G. W. Evans and S. Honkapohja (2005), p. 566.

25 Committee on Oversight and Government Reform (2008), p. 37.

3: RIGHTS

1 J. Rawls (1971), p. 29.

2 J. Rawls (1971), pp. 3–4.

3 W. J. Clinton (29 Sept. 1999).

4 R. Nozick (1990) pp. 32–3.

5 J. Rousseau (1761), p. 97.

6 G. Hardin (1968).

7 United Nations (1948).

8   Schenk v. United States (1919).
9   R. Dworkin (1977), p. xi.
10 A. MacIntyre (2013), p. 83.

4: FROM CIVIL RIGHTS TO EXPRESSIVE IDENTITY

1   Planned Parenthood v. Casey (1991), p. 851.
2   M. Walzer (2019).
3   K. R. Minogue (1963), p. 1.
4   Mermaids (undated).
5   Occupy London (17 Oct. 2011).
6   R. Milkman, S. Luce and P. Lewis (2013), pp. 8–9.
7   M. Crippa et al. (2019).
8   W. Kopp (2003), p. 4.
9   https://list25.com/25-worst-lottery-winner-horror-stories-cautionary-tales/
10 The academic evidence that at some point well-being ceases to rise with income is long-standing, but more recently academics have also found that, beyond that income level, more money actually reduces well-being. See, for example, Paul Nolan's *Happy Ever After* (2019). Professor Nolan finds the peak of happiness occurs at the income range £40–59,000 a year.
11 A survey of 500 people earning over £100,000 a year found that two-thirds admitted to significant problems with their relationships, which we know are fundamental for well-being. In contrast, only a fifth in the general population admits to such problems. It is reported in A. Holder (23 Jan. 2020).
12 E. Zimmerman (2020), citing research by the Hazelden Betty Ford Foundation. A chilling vignette in Zimmerman's book is the funeral of one of the partners, at which the mourners are busy on their smartphones.
13 N. MacGregor (2018), Chapter 8.

5: THE RISE AND FALL OF THE PATERNAL STATE

1   See N. Westcott (2020).
2   H. Morrison (1933).

3 British Transport Commission (1955), p. 5.
4 A. King and I. Crewe (2014), Chapter 13.
5 In T. Collins (12 Apr. 2006); House of Commons Public Accounts
   Committee (14 Jan. 2009), p. 14.
6 Quoted in P. Clark et al. (27 Mar. 2020).
7 C. Drosten quoted in R. Schmitz (27 Mar. 2020).
8 Edelman (2019).

6: SHIFTING POLITICAL TECTONIC PLATES

1 R. Todd quoted by N. Kinnock in M. Rutherford (2 Oct. 1987).
2 R. J. Gordon (2016).
3 J. Callaghan, quoted in Labour Party Annual Conference Report
   (1976), p. 176.
4 K. Clarke in S. Payne (10 Jan. 2020).

7: HOW LABOUR LOST THE WORKING CLASS

1 A. Rae (5 Nov. 2019).
2 House of Commons Library (17 Apr. 2020).
3 N. Dempsey (6 Feb. 2017). Note that, unlike for some constituencies, these are estimates based on Chris Hanretty's model.
4 Quoted in BBC (14 Dec. 2019).
5 P. G. J. Pulzer (1967), p. 98.
6 A. McDonnell and C. Curtis (17 Dec. 2019).
7 Ibid.
8 Ibid.
9 P. Bolton (27 Nov. 2012), p. 14. The report notes that 'Overall
   participation in higher education increased from 3.4% in 1950, to
   8.4% in 1970 [most of whom will have been born around 1950],
   19.3% in 1990 and 33% in 2000.'
10 E. Fieldhouse and G. Evans (2020), p. 13.
11 A. Tyson and S. Maniam (9 Nov. 2016).
12 R. Florida (28 Nov. 2018). The data on occupation and voting
   behaviour is from the same source – manicurists are the occupation
   least, and welders most, likely to support Trump.
13 M. Young (29 June 2001).
14 N. Kinnock (7 June 1983) in S. Ratcliffe (2016).
15 P. Mandelson (Oct. 1999) in S. Ratcliffe (2016).

16 J. Carey (1992), p. 152.
17 V. Woolf (1924), p. 15.
18 S. L. McFall (2012) Table 1.
19 A. Chua (2018), p. 5.

8: OUR COMMUNITARIAN NATURE

1 A. H. Maslow (1943).
2 See M. E. P. Seligman (2011); for a more recent study that reaches the same conclusion see R. Layard (2020).
3 E. Burke (1790), pp. 68–9.
4 G. W. F. Hegel (1820).
5 A. de Tocqueville (1862) p. 128.
6 K. Marx (1859).
7 A. Etzioni (2003).
8 N. A. Christakis (2019), p. 418.
9 The Asian Republican (21 Sept. 2016).
10 G. Marwell and R. E. Ames (1981), p. 309.
11 Peter Theil – subtitle of Future Fund manifesto, 2011.

9: COMMUNITARIAN GOVERNANCE

1 E. Ostrom (1991).
2 See D. S. Wilson (2020).
3 T. Philippon (2019) shows how corporate lobbying of Congress has eroded competition in the USA.
4 See, for example, C. O'Neil (2011).
5 K. Pickett and R. Wilkinson (2010) report many of these correlations, asserting without specific evidence that causation runs from income inequality to the other variable.
6 B. Herrmann, C. Thöni and S. Gächter (2008).
7 J. Henrich (2017), p. 123.
8 I. L. Janis (1972).
9 S. E. Ambrose (1984), p. 638.
10 R. F. Kennedy (1999), pp. 26–7 and 35–6.
11 Ibid., pp. 85–6.

10: COMMUNITARIAN POLITICS

1 A. Jackson quoted in R. V. Remini (1984), p. 273.
2 G. S. Becker (1973), p. 814.
3 J. Sumption (2019), p. 66.
4 C. Binham and J. Croft (9 Mar. 2020).
5 C. Attlee, quoted in V. Bogdanor (1981), p. 35.
6 E. Burke (1874), p. 11.
7 Ibid.
8 Ibid.
9 P. Maguire (27 Feb. 2020); House of Commons Library (2020).
10 House of Commons Library (2019).
11 N. MacGregor (2018).
12 The matter is brilliantly elucidated in M. Burbridge, A. Briggs, and M. Reiss (2020).

11: COMMUNITARIANISM, MARKETS AND BUSINESS

1 H. A. Simon (1962), p. 470.
2 A. Doyle (4 Mar. 2016).
3 M. M. Blair and L. A. Stout (1999), p. 278.
4 J. A. Kay (10 Nov. 2015).
5 Business Roundtable (19 Aug. 2019).
6 A. Smith (1776), p. 17.
7 J. P. Morgan (1912), p. 2.

COMMUNITIES OF PLACE

1 Jacobs (1961).
2 Office for National Statistics (19 Dec. 2019a).
3 Office for National Statistics (19 Dec. 2019b).
4 P. Brien (13 Dec. 2019).
5 J. Gramlich (6 Nov. 2019).
6 F. Perraudin (3 Oct. 2019).
7 R. Yehuda et al. (2005).
8 Putnam (2015), p.114.
9 H. Cottam (2018), and subsequent discussion with the author.

10 The quotation is from a public lecture given at the University of Southampton in 2002. We are indebted to Richard Seebohm for recounting it.

11 H. Cottam (2018), p. 13.

12 Ibid., p. 8.

13 See R. D. Putnam (2015) and J. J. Heckman (2012).

14 R. D. Putnam (2015), p. 182.

15 A. Goldstein (2018).

16 A. Shafique (13 Feb. 2019).

EPILOGUE: SHELTER FROM THE STORM

1 T. Buck (8 Sept. 2017).

2 L. Kendall (14 Mar. 2020).

3 S. Murphy (25 Mar. 2020).

4 Thucydides, Chapter VII (430BC).

Further Reading

As we complete this book, we see encouraging signs that the half-century of extreme individualism is coming to an end. We have just had an opportunity to read Jonathan Sacks's newly published *Morality* (2020). Lord Sacks's background – for many years he was Chief Rabbi of the Commonwealth – could hardly be more different from our careers as professional economists, and yet we have not only arrived at much the same place but record a number of similar milestones on the way. Ragu Rajan, who earned widespread displeasure when as Chief Economist of the International Monetary Fund in 2005 he warned of the systemic risks building up in the global financial system, has more recently turned his attention to *The Third Pillar* (2019), the importance of community of place in the effective functioning of economies and societies. And we await Michael Sandel's echo of Michael Young's identification of the hubris of meritocracy and the nakedness of the underclass it leaves behind in *The Tyranny of Merit* (2020).

Nicholas Christakis's *Blueprint: The Evolutionary Origins of a Good Society* (2019) decisively affirms that humans are intrinsically and distinctively prosocial. Christakis's book is usefully read alongside Joseph Henrich's *The Secret of our Success* (2017) and Hugo Mercier and Dan Sperber's *The Enigma of Reason* (2017). These recent works draw on genetics, sociology, psychology and decision science to direct us towards an understanding of how the combination of cooperation and competition has shaped not just our communities but our economies.

On leaving the Bank of England after seven years as Governor, Mark Carney took space in the *Economist* (16 April 2020) to emphasize the need to rethink the relationships between finance, business and community. Colin Mayer's *Prosperity: Better Business Makes the Greater Good* (2018), and Rebecca Henderson's *Reimagining*

Capitalism in a World on Fire (2020) both powerfully capture the new shift in corporate purpose from the mantra of shareholder value, as does Judy Samuelson's *The Six New Rules of Business* (2021).

This turning of the intellectual tide is already being reflected in fresh thinking within the political parties. In *Remaking One Nation* (2020), Nick Timothy, Theresa May's principal adviser until her inept election campaign, has mapped out a communitarian path for the British Conservative Party. David Skelton's *Little Platoons* (2019) develops similar themes. Ed West's *Small Men on the Wrong Side of History* (2020) does so in an engagingly lighter vein. Jesse Norman MP's recent works on *Edmund Burke* (2013) and *Adam Smith* (2018) are intended not just to offer a fresh account of these historical figures – dispelling any notion of Smith as precursor of Ivan Boesky and Gordon Gekko – but to set out a vision for modern politics on the centre-right.

As Britain's Labour Party emerges from the intellectual poverty of the Corbyn era, a few works have begun to set out a road ahead. *The New Serfdom* (2018), by Angela Eagle MP and Imran Ahmed, begins the process of describing a twenty-first-century economic philosophy for the centre-left, and David Swift's *A Left for Itself* (2019) is a powerful response to the current preoccupation with identity politics. But we feel no hesitation in recommending Paul's *The Future of Capitalism* (2018) to those on the left who perceive the need for new directions, and John's *Radical Uncertainty: Decision-making for an Unknowable Future* (2020), co-authored with Mervyn King, to those who perceive that, while economic orthodoxy cannot be trusted, Marxism is not the alternative.

That theme of the loss of direction on the left is well covered by some American writers. Mark Lilla's *The Once and Future Liberal* (2017) is not only an effective exposition but has a title which resonates with our own feelings; we appreciate the observation of the Danish Social Democrat leader and now Prime Minister Mette Frederiksen to voters that 'you didn't leave us: we left you'. David Goodhart's *The Road to Somewhere* (2017) is in similar vein. Michael Lind's *The New Class War* (2020) is a guide to the relationship between the rise of meritocracy and the rise of Trump, and Patrick Deneen's *Why Liberalism Failed* (2018) is a further discussion of the same history.

Lord Sacks describes how reading Alasdair Macintyre's *After Virtue* (1981) reset his thinking on communitarian lines. We each had separately a similar experience, and, although this book is not the easiest introduction to communitarian philosophy, and Macintyre's views on the market economy are very different from ours, we hope that others may also find inspiration there. John's *The Truth About Markets* (2003) is a description of how markets and community are mutually supportive rather than mutually antagonistic which, we believe, has stood up well to the political and economic events of the past two decades.

And, over a longer period, *Habits of the Heart* (1985), essays in sociology which capture US communities of the early 1980s, Christopher Lasch's *The Culture of the Narcissism* (1979) and *The Revolt of the Elites* (1995), which read even more persuasively now than they did then, and Robert Putnam's classic *Bowling Alone* (2000) have retained their contemporary relevance. They are each essential references on the communitarian bookshelf.

Bibliography

Altig, D. E. and Smith, B. D. *Evolution and Procedures in Central Banking* (Cambridge: Cambridge University Press, 2003)

Ambrose, S. E. *Eisenhower: The President: Volume Two, 1952–1969* (London: George Allen and Unwin, 1984)

Angelou, M. *All God's Children Need Traveling Shoes* (New York: Random House, 1986)

Anscombe, G. E. M. 'Modern Moral Philosophy', *Philosophy*, Vol. 33, No. 124 (1958), 1–19

Aristotle. Jowett, B. (trans.). *Politics* (350BC)

Arrow, K. J. 'A Difficulty in the Concept of Social Welfare', *Journal of Political Economy*, Vol. 58, No. 4 (1950), 328–46

Arrow, K. J. and Debreu, G. 'Existence of an Equilibrium for a Competitive Economy', *Econometrica*, Vol. 22, No. 3 (1954), 265–90

Arrow, K. J. and Hahn, F. H. *General Competitive Analysis* (Amsterdam: North Holland Publishing, 1983)

The Asian Republican. 'Yale University – Full Version – New Videos of the Halloween Email Protest', YouTube (21 Sept. 2016), https://www.youtube.com/watch?v=hiMVx2C5_Wg accessed 20 Apr. 2020

Associated Press. 'Trump in Nevada: "I Love the Poorly Educated"', YouTube (23 Feb. 2016), https://www.youtube.com/watch?v=Vpdt7omPoao accessed 20 Apr. 2020

BBC. 'Wishy-washy Centrism Wrong for Labour, Warns Lord Hain', BBC News (14 Dec. 2019), https://www.bbc.co.uk/news/election-2019-50793959 accessed 20 Apr. 2020

Becker, G. S. 'A Theory of Marriage: Part I', *Journal of Political Economy*, Vol. 81, No. 4 (1973), 813–46

Becker, G. S. *The Economic Approach to Human Behavior* (Chicago: University of Chicago Press, 1976)

Bellah, R. N. et al. *Habits of the Heart: Individualism and Commitment in American Life* (Berkeley: University of California Press, 1985)

Bentham, J. *The Works of Jeremy Bentham, Vol. 2 (Judicial Procedure, Anarchical Fallacies, works on Taxation)* (1843)

Bentham, J., Burns, J. H. and Hart, H. L. A. (eds.). *A Comment on the Commentaries and A Fragment on Government: The Collected Works of Jeremy Bentham* (London: OUP, 1977)

Besley, T. and S. Dray, 2020, *Responsiveness during the COVID-19 Crisis: Does Free Media Make a Difference?* Working Paper, STICERD, London School of Economics.

Binham, C. and Croft, J. 'Barclays: The Legal Fight over a Company's "Controlling Mind"', *Financial Times* (9 Mar. 2020)

Blair, M. M. and Stout, L. A. 'A Team Production Theory of Corporate Law', *Virginia Law Review*, Vol. 85, No. 2 (1999), 248–328

Bogdanor, V. *The People and the Party System: The Referendum and Electoral Reform in British Politics* (Cambridge: CUP, 1981)

Bolton, P. 'Education: Historical Statistics', House of Commons Library (27 Nov. 2012)

Brien, P. 'Public Spending by Country and Region', House of Commons Library (13 Dec. 2019), https://commonslibrary.parliament.uk/research-briefings/sno4033/ accessed 3 Apr. 2020

British Transport Commission. 'Modernisation and Re-equipment of British Railways' (London: Curwen Press, 1955)

Buck, T. 'Germany's Club Culture Offers Clue to Political Consensus', *Financial Times* (8 Sept. 2017)

Burbridge, M., Briggs, A. and Reiss, M. *Citizenship in a Networked Age: An Agenda for Rebuilding Our Civic Ideals* (Templeton Foundation, 2020)

Burke, E. *Reflections on the Revolution in France* (1790)

Burke, E. *Selected Works of Edmund Burke* (Oxford: Clarendon Press, 1874)

Business Roundtable. 'Business Roundtable Redefines the Purpose of a Corporation to Promote "An Economy That Serves All Americans"', businessroundtable.org (19 Aug. 2019), https://www.businessroundtable.org/business-roundtable-redefines-the-purpose-of-a-corporation-to-promote-an-economy-that-serves-all-americans accessed 3 Apr. 2020

Carey, J. *The Intellectuals and the Masses: Pride and Prejudice among the Literary Intelligentsia 1880–1939* (London: Faber and Faber, 1992)

Carney, M. 'Mark Carney on How the Economy Must Yield to Human Values', *The Economist* (16 Apr. 2020)

Chakrabortty, A. 'One Blunt Heckler Has Revealed Just How Much the UK Economy is Failing Us', *Guardian* (10 Jan. 2017)

Christakis, N. A. *Blueprint: The Evolutionary Origins of a Good Society* (London: Little, Brown Spark, 2019)

Chua, A. *Political Tribes: Group Instinct and the Fate of Nations* (London: Bloomsbury, 2018)

Clark, P. et al. 'How the UK got Coronavirus Testing Wrong', *Financial Times* (27 Mar. 2020)

Clinton, W. J. 'Remarks by the President at Presentation of the National Medal of the Arts and the National Humanities Medal' (29 Sept. 1999), https://clintonwhitehouse4.archives.gov/WH/New/html/19990929.html accessed 2 Apr. 2020

Collier, P. *The Future of Capitalism: Facing the New Anxieties* (London: Allen Lane, 2018)

Collins, J. *How the Mighty Fall: And Why Some Companies Never Give In* (London: Random House, 2009)

Collins, J. and Porras, J. I. *Built to Last: Successful Habits of Visionary Companies* (London: Random House, 2005; first published 1994)

Collins, T. 'NHS Focus: Open Letter: Questions That Need to be Answered', *Computer Weekly* (12 Apr. 2006), https://www.computerweekly.com/feature/NHS-Focus-Open-Letter-Questions-that-need-to-be-answered accessed 2 Apr. 2020

The Committee for the Prize in Economic Sciences in Memory of Alfred Nobel. 'Gary S. Becker – Facts' (1992)

Committee on Oversight and Government Reform. 'The Financial Crisis and the Role of Federal Regulators', House of Representatives (23 Oct. 2008)

Cottam, H. *Radical Help* (London: Virago, 2018)

Crippa, M. et al. *Fossil CO_2 and GHG Emissions of All World Countries*, Joint Research Centre (Luxembourg: Publications Office of the European Union, 2019)

Crosland, A. *The Future of Socialism* (London: Jonathan Cape, 1956)

Crow, D. 'Two Executives Charged over Illegal Kickback Scheme at Valeant', *Financial Times* (17 Nov. 2016)

Dempsey, N. 'EU Referendum: Constituency Results' (6 Feb. 2017), available at https://commonslibrary.parliament.uk/parliament-and-elections/elections-elections/brexit-votes-by-constituency/ accessed 20 Apr. 2020

Deneen, P. J. *Why Liberalism Failed* (New Haven: Yale University Press, 2018)

De Tocqueville, A. *Democracy in America* (1862)

Doyle, A. 'Management and Organization at Medium', *Medium* (4 Mar. 2016), https://blog.medium.com/management-and-organization-at-medium-2228cc9d93e9 accessed 3 Apr. 2020

Dworkin, R. *Taking Rights Seriously* (Cambridge, MA: HUP, 1977)

Eagle, A. and Ahmed, I. *The New Serfdom: The Triumph of Conservative Ideas and How to Defeat Them* (London: Biteback Publishing, 2018)

Easterbrook, F. H. and Fischel, D. R. *The Economic Structure of Corporate Law* (Cambridge, MA: Harvard University Press, 1996)

Edelman. '2019 Edelman Trust Barometer' (2019), https://www.edelman.com/sites/g/files/aatuss191/files/2019–02/2019_Edelman_Trust_Barometer_Global_Report.pdf accessed 2 Apr. 2020

Etzioni, A. 'Communitarianism', in Christensen, K. and Levinson, D. (eds.) *Encyclopedia of Community: From the Village to the Virtual World, Vol. 1, A–D* (Sage Publications, 2003), 224–8. Available at SSRN: https://ssrn.com/abstract=2157152

Ferguson, A. *An Essay on the History of Civil Society* (1767)

Fieldhouse, E. and Evans, G. *Electoral Shocks: The Volatile Voter in a Turbulent World* (Oxford: OUP, 2020)

Florida, R. 'Why is Your State Red or Blue? Look to the Dominant Occupational Class', *CityLab* (28 Nov. 2018), https://www.citylab.com/life/2018/11/state-voting-patterns-occupational-class-data-politics/575047/ accessed 20 Apr. 2020

Fortune. 'World's Most Admired Companies' (2020), https://fortune.com/worlds-most-admired-companies/ accessed 2 Apr. 2020

Friedman, M. 'The Social Responsibility of Business is to Increase Its Profits', *The New York Times Magazine* (13 Sept. 1970)

Friedman, M. and Savage, L. J. 'The Utility Analysis of Choices Involving Risk', *Journal of Political Economy*, Vol. 56, No. 4 (1948), 279–304

Glendon, M. A. *Rights Talk: The Impoverishment of Political Discourse* (New York: Free Press, 1991)

Goldman Sachs, 'Code of Business Conduct and Ethics', https://www.goldmansachs.com/investor-relations/corporate-governance/corporate-governance-documents/code-of-business-conduct-and-ethics.pdf accessed 20 Apr. 2020

Goldstein, A. *Janesville: An American Story* (New York: Simon and Schuster, 2018)

Goodhart, D. *The Road to Somewhere: The Populist Revolt and the Future of Politics* (London: Hurst, 2017)

Gordon, R. J. *The Rise and Fall of American Growth* (Princeton: Princeton University Press, 2016)

Gramlich, J. 'East Germany Has Narrowed Economic Gap with West Germany since Fall of Communism, but Still Lags', *Pew Research Centre* (6 Nov. 2019), https://www.pewresearch.org/fact-tank/2019/11/06/east-germany-has-narrowed-economic-gap-with-west-germany-since-fall-of-communism-but-still-lags/ accessed 3 Apr. 2020

Greene, B. 'A $100 Million Idea: Use Greed for Good', *Chicago Tribune* (15 Dec. 1986)

Handy, C. 'What's a Business For?', *Harvard Business Review*, Vol. 80, No. 2 (2002) 49–55

Hardin, G. 'The Tragedy of the Commons', *Science*, Vol. 162, No. 3859 (1968), 1243–8

Heckman, J. J. 'Promoting Social Mobility', *Boston Review* (1 Sept. 2012), http://bostonreview.net/forum/promoting-social-mobility-james-heckman accessed 21 Apr. 2020

Hegel, G. W. F. *Grundlinien der Philosophie des Rechts* (1820)

Henderson, J. *Reimagining Capitalism in a World on Fire* (New York: PublicAffairs, 2020)

Henrich, J. *The Secret of Our Success: How Culture is Driving Human Evolution, Domesticating Our Species, and Making Us Smarter* (Princeton: Princeton University Press, 2017)

Herrmann, B., Thöni, C. and Gächter, S. 'Antisocial Punishment across Societies', *Science*, Vol. 319, No. 5868 (2008), 1362–7

Hoffman, J. 'Johnson & Johnson Ordered to Pay $572 Million in Landmark Opioid Trial', *The New York Times* (26 Aug. 2019)

Holder, A. 'The "Salary Sweet Spot" that Could Save Your Relationship', *Daily Telegraph* (23 Jan. 2020)

House of Commons Library, 'Membership of UK Political Parties' (9 Aug. 2019), https://commonslibrary.parliament.uk/research-briefings/sn05125/ accessed 3 Apr. 2020)

House of Commons Library, 'General Election 2019: Full Results and Analysis' (28 Jan. 2020), https://commonslibrary.parliament.uk/research-briefings/cbp-8749/ accessed 3 Apr. 2020

House of Commons Library, '1918–2019 Election Results by GE' (17 Apr. 2020), https://commonslibrary.parliament.uk/research-briefings/cbp-8647/ accessed 20 Apr. 2020

House of Commons Public Accounts Committee. 'The National Programme for IT in the NHS: Progress since 2006: Second Report of Session 2008–09' (14 Jan. 2009)

Jacobs, J. *The Death and Life of Great American Cities* (New York: Random House, 1961)

Janis, I. L. *Victims of Groupthink: A Psychological Study of Foreign Policy Decisions and Fiascoes* (New York: Houghton Mifflin, 1972)

Jefferson, T. *Memoir, Correspondence, and Miscellanies: From the Papers of Thomas Jefferson* (1829)

Jensen, M. C. and Meckling, W. H. 'Theory of the Firm: Managerial Behavior, Agency Costs and Ownership Structure', *Journal of Financial Economics*, Vol. 3, No. 4 (1976) 305–60

Kay, J. A. *The Truth About Markets: Why Some Nations are Rich but Most Remain Poor* (London: Allen Lane, 2003)

Kay, J. A. 'Shareholders Think They Own the Company – They are Wrong', *Financial Times* (10 Nov. 2015)

Kay, J. A. and King, M. A. *Radical Uncertainty: Decision-making for an Unknowable Future* (London: Bridge Street Press, 2020)

Kendall, L. 'Fixing Social Care is More Important than Potholes', *Financial Times* (14 Mar. 2020)

Kennedy, J. F. 'Inaugural Address', John F. Kennedy Presidential Library and Museum (20 Jan. 1961), https://www.jfklibrary.org/learn/about-jfk/historic-speeches/inaugural-address accessed 20 Apr. 2020

Kennedy, R. F. *Thirteen Days: A Memoir of the Cuban Missile Crisis* (New York: Norton, 1999)

Keynes, J. M. *The General Theory of Employment, Interest and Money* (London: Macmillan and Co., 1936)

King, A. and Crewe, I. *The Blunders of Our Governments* (Oneworld Publications, 2014), e-version

Kopp, W. *One Day, All Children . . .: The Unlikely Triumph of Teach for America and What I Learned along the Way* (Cambridge, MA: PublicAffairs, 2003)

Kozarich, D. 'Mylan's EpiPen Pricing Crossed Ethical Boundaries', *Fortune* (27 Sept. 2016)

Kuchler, H. et al. 'Opioid Executive Admits to "No Morals" ahead of Prison Term', *Financial Times* (23 Jan. 2020)

Labour Party Annual Conference Report (1976)

Lasch, C. *The Culture of Narcissism: American Life in an Age of Diminishing Expectations* (New York: W. W. Norton & Company, 1979)

Lasch, C. *The Revolt of the Elites and the Betrayal of Democracy* (New York: W. W. Norton & Company, 1995)

Layard, R. *Can We be Happier?: Evidence and Ethics* (London: Penguin, 2020)

Levinson, M. *An Extraordinary Time: The End of the Postwar Boom and the Return of the Ordinary Economy* (London: Random House, 2016)

Lilla, M. *The Once and Future Liberal: After Identity Politics* (New York: HarperCollins, 2017)

Limbaugh, R. 'The Most Telling Moment of Obama's Presidency: "You Didn't Build That"', *The Rush Limbaugh Show* (24 July 2012), https://www.rushlimbaugh.com/daily/2012/07/24/the_most_telling_moment_of_obama_s_presidency_you_didn_t_build_that/ accessed 6 Apr. 2020

Lind, M. *The New Class War: Saving Democracy from the Metropolitan Elite* (London: Atlantic Books, 2020)

MacGregor, N. *Living with the Gods: On Beliefs and Peoples* (London: Allen Lane, 2018)

MacIntyre, A. *After Virtue* (London: Bloomsbury, 2013)

Macmurray, J. *Persons in Relation* (London: Faber, 1961)

Maguire, P. 'Long-Bailey's Shift to Attack Mode Shows What Awaits Starmer if He Wins', *Guardian* (27 Feb. 2020)

Marwell, G. and Ames, R. E. 'Economists Free Ride, Does Anyone Else? Experiments on the Provision of Public Goods, IV', *Journal of Public Economics*, Vol. 15, No. 3 (1981), 295–310

Marx, K. *Preface, A Contribution to the Critique of Political Economy* (1859), https://www.marxists.org/archive/marx/works/1859/critique-pol-economy/preface.htm accessed 2 Apr. 2020

Maslow, A. H. 'A Theory of Human Motivation', *Psychological Review*, Vol. 50, No. 4 (1943) 370–96

Matthews, R. C. O. 'Why Has Britain Had Full Employment since the War?', *Economic Journal*, Vol. 78, No. 311 (1968) 555–69

Mayer, C. *Prosperity: Better Business Makes the Greater Good* (Oxford University Press) 2018.

McDonnell, A. and Curtis, C. 'How Britain Voted in the 2019 General Election', *YouGov* (17 Dec. 2019), https://yougov.co.uk/topics/politics/articles-reports/2019/12/17/how-britain-voted-2019-general-election accessed 20 Apr. 2020

McFall, S. L. (ed.). *Understanding Society: Findings 2012* (Colchester: Institute for Social and Economic Research, University of Essex, 2012)

Mercier, H. and Sperber, D. *The Enigma of Reason: A New Theory of Human Understanding* (London: Allen Lane, 2017)

Merck, G. W. 'Medicine is for the Patient, not the Profits' (1 Dec. 1950), https://www.merck.com/about/our-people/gw-merck-doc.pdf accessed 2 Apr. 2020

Mermaids, 'Professionals', https://mermaidsuk.org.uk/professionals/ accessed 20 Apr. 2020

Milkman, R., Luce, S. and Lewis, P. *Changing the Subject: A Bottom-up Account of Occupy Wall Street in New York City*, The Murphy Institute (2013)

Minogue, K. R. *The Liberal Mind* (New York: Random House, 1963)

Morgan, J. P. 'J. P. Morgan's Testimony: The Justification of Wall Street' (1912), available at https://memory.loc.gov/service/gdc/scd0001/2006/20060517001te/20060517001te.pdf accessed 3 Apr. 2020

Morrison, H. *Socialisation of Transport* (HMSO: 1933)

Murphy, S. 'More than 500,000 People Sign Up to be NHS Volunteers', *Guardian* (25 Mar. 2020)

National Centre of Health Statistics, *Health, United States, 2018: Table 009: Death Rates for Suicide, by Sex, Race, Hispanic Origin, and Age: United States, Selected Years 1950–2017* (2018), https://www.cdc.gov/nchs/data/hus/2018/009.pdf accessed 20 Apr. 2020

Nixon, R. M. 'Second Inaugural Address of Richard Milhous Nixon', The Avalon Project (20 Jan. 1973), https://avalon.law.yale.edu/20th_century/nixon2.asp accessed 6 Apr. 2020

Nolan, P. *Happily Ever After: Escaping the Myth of the Perfect Life* (London: Allen Lane, 2019)

Norman, J. *Adam Smith: What He Thought, and Why It Matters* (London: Penguin, 2018)

Norman, J. *Edmund Burke: The Visionary Who Invented Modern Politics* (London: William Collins, 2013)

Nozick, R. *Anarchy, State and Utopia* (Oxford: Basil Blackwell Ltd., 1990; first published 1974)

Obama, B. H. 'Remarks by the President at a Campaign Event in Roanoke, Virginia', Office of the Press Secretary (13 July 2012), https://obamawhitehouse.archives.gov/the-press-office/2012/07/13/remarks-president-campaign-event-roanoke-virginia accessed 6 Apr. 2020

Occupy London, 'Occupy London Stock Exchange – the Initial Statement', *Guardian* (17 Oct. 2011)

Office for National Statistics. 'Headline Estimates of Personal Well-being from the Annual Population Survey (APS)' (23 Oct. 2019)

Office for National Statistics, 'Regional Economic Activity by Gross Domestic Product, UK: 1998 to 2018' (19 Dec. 2019a), https://www.ons.gov.uk/economy/grossdomesticproductgdp/bulletins/regionaleconomicactivitybygrossdomesticproductuk/1998to2018#gross-domestic-product-per-head-for-nuts3-local-areas-1998-to-2018 accessed 3 Apr. 2020

Office for National Statistics. 'Regional Gross Domestic Product all NUTS Level Regions' (19 Dec. 2019b), https://www.ons.gov.uk/economy/grossdomesticproductgdp/datasets/regionalgrossdomesticproductallnutslevelregions accessed 3 Apr. 2020

Office for National Statistics. 'Suicides in the UK, 1981 to 2018' (3 Sept. 2019), https://www.ons.gov.uk/peoplepopulationandcommunity/birthsdeathsandmarriages/deaths/datasets/suicidesintheunitedkingdomreferencetables accessed 20 Apr. 2020

O'Neil, C. 'Working with Larry Summers (Part 2)', mathbabe.com (24 June 2011), https://mathbabe.org/2011/06/24/working-with-larry-summers-part-2/ accessed 2 Apr. 2020

Ostrom, E. *Governing the Commons: The Evolution of Institutions for Collective Action* (Cambridge: Cambridge University Press, 1991)

Payne, S. 'Lunch with the FT: Ken Clarke: "Do We Carry On with Crash, Bang, Wallop Nationalism?"', *Financial Times* (10 Jan. 2020)

Perraudin, F. 'UK Should Compensate Wales for "Reducing it to Poverty" – Plaid Cymru', *Guardian* (3 Oct. 2019)

Peters, T. 'The Brand Called You', *Fast Company* (31 Aug. 1997), https://www.fastcompany.com/28905/brand-called-you accessed 20 Apr. 2020

Philippon, T. *The Great Reversal: How America Gave Up on Free Markets* (Cambridge, MA: The Belknap Press, 2019)

Philosophy Department at San José University. 'An Open Letter to Professor Michael Sandel' (29 Apr. 2013), available at https://www.chronicle.com/article/The-Document-an-Open-Letter/138937 accessed 20 Apr. 2020

Pickett, K. and Wilkinson, R. *The Spirit Level: Why Equality is Better for Everyone* (London: Penguin, 2010)

Planned Parenthood of Southeastern Pennsylvania et al. v. Casey, Governor of Pennsylvania, et al. *Certiorari to the United States Court of Appeals for the Third Circuit* (1991)

Platt, E. 'Adam Neumann's $1.6bn WeWork Exit Package Could Get Sweeter', *Financial Times* (24 Dec. 2019)

Platt, E. 'WeWork's Adam Neumann Returns Controversial $5.9m Payment', *Financial Times* (5 Sept. 2019)

Pulzer, P. G. J. *Political Representation and Elections* (London: Harper-Collins, 1967)

Putnam, R. D. *Bowling Alone: The Collapse and Revival of American Community* (New York: Simon and Schuster, 2000)

Putnam, R. D. *Our Kids: The American Dream in Crisis* (New York: Simon and Schuster, 2015)

Rae, A. 'I Ranked Every UK Constituency by Deprivation and then Coloured Them by Party Affiliation – for Fun!', *CityMetric* (5 Nov. 2019), https://www.citymetric.com/politics/i-ranked-every-uk-constituency-deprivation-and-then-coloured-them-party-affiliation-fun accessed 20 Apr. 2020

Rajan, R. *The Third Pillar: The Revival of Community in a Polarised World* (London: William Collins, 2019)

Ramsey, F. P. 'A Mathematical Theory of Saving', *Economic Journal*, Vol. 38, No. 152 (1928) 543–59

Ratcliffe, S. (ed.) *Oxford Essential Quotations* (Oxford: Oxford University Press, 2016)

Rawls, J. *A Theory of Justice* (Cambridge, MA: Belknap Press, 1971)

Remini, R. V. 'Andrew Jackson: The Course of American Democracy, 1833–1845' (Baltimore, MA: Johns Hopkins University Press, 1984)

Rousseau, J. *A Discourse upon the Origin and Foundation of the Inequality among Mankind* (1761)

Rutherford, M. 'Politics Today: Waiting for the Country to Turn Conservative – Labour at Brighton', *Financial Times* (2 Oct. 1987)

Sacks, J. *Morality: Restoring the Common Good in Divided Times* (London: Hodder and Stoughton, 2020)

Samuelson, J. *The Six New Rules of Business: Creating Real Value in a Changing World* (Berrett-Koehler Publishers, 2021)

Sandel, M. J. *The Tyranny of Merit: What's Become of the Common Good* (London: Penguin, 2020)

Sandel, M. J. *What Money Can't Buy: The Moral Limits of Markets* (London: Allen Lane, 2012)

Santos, H. C. et al. 'Global Increases in Individualism', *Psychological Science*, Vol. 28, No. 9 (2017), 1228–39

Sargent, T. J., Evans, G. W. and Honkapohja, S. 'An Interview with Thomas J. Sargent', *Macroeconomic Dynamics*, Vol. 9 (2005), 561–83

Schenk v. United States, 249 U.S. 47 (1919)

Schmitz, R. 'Behind Germany's Relatively Low COVID-19 Fatality Rate', *NPR All Things Considered* (27 Mar. 2020), https://www.npr.org/2020/03/25/821591044/behind-germanys-relatively-low-covid-19-fatality-rate accessed 2 Apr. 2020

Seligman, M. E. P. *Flourish: A Visionary New Understanding of Happiness and Well-being* (New York: Free Press, 2011)

Shafique, A. 'If the UK Wants a Quality Vocational Educational System, It Should Take Inspiration from Switzerland', *RSA* (13 Feb. 2019), https://www.thersa.org/discover/publications-and-articles/rsa-blogs/2019/02/what-uk-vocational-education-can-learn-from-switzerland accessed 3 Apr. 2020

Sidgwick, G. *The Method of Ethics* (London: Macmillan, 1962)

Simon, H. A. 'The Architecture of Complexity', *Proceedings of the American Philosophical Society*, Vol. 106, No. 6 (1962) 467–82

Singer, P. 'Famine, Affluence, and Morality', *Philosophy and Public Affairs*, Vol. 1, No. 3 (1972) 229–43

Skelton, D. *Little Platoons: How a Revived One Nation Can Empower England's Forgotten Towns and Redraw the Political Map* (London: Biteback Publishing, 2019)

Smith, A. *The Theory of Moral Sentiments* (1759)

Smith, A. *An Inquiry into the Nature and Causes of the Wealth of Nations* (1776)

Sombart, W. Husbands, C. T. (ed.). *Why is There no Socialism in the United States?* (White Plains: M. E. Sharpe, Inc., 1976)

Sumption, J. *Trials of the State: Law and the Decline of Politics* (London: Profile, 2019)

Swift, D. *A Left for Itself: Left-Wing Hobbyists and the Rise of Identity Radicalism* (Winchester: Zero Books, 2019)

Thucydides. Crawley, A. (trans. 2004). *The History of the Peloponnesian War* (430BC)

Timothy, N. *Remaking One Nation: The Future of Conservatism* (Cambridge: Polity Press, 2020)

Twenge, J. M. et al. 'Age, Period, and Cohort Trends in Mood Disorder Indicators and Suicide-related Outcomes in a Nationally Representative Dataset, 2005–2017', *Journal of Abnormal Psychology*, Vol. 128, No. 3 (2019), 185–99

Tyson, A. and Maniam, S. 'Behind Trump's Victory: Divisions by Race, Gender, Education', Pew Research Center (9 Nov. 2016), https://www.pewresearch.org/fact-tank/2016/11/09/behind-trumps-victory-divisions-by-race-gender-education/ accessed 20 Apr. 2020)

United Nations. *The Universal Declaration of Human Rights* (1948)

Waldfogel, J. *Scroogenomics: Why You Shouldn't Buy Presents for the Holidays* (Princeton: Princeton University Press, 2009)

Wall Street Journal Editorial, '"You Didn't Build That": On the President's Burst of Ideological Candor', *Wall Street Journal* (19 July 2012)

Walzer, M. *Spheres of Justice: A Defense of Pluralism and Equality* (New York: Basic Books, 1983)

Walzer, M. *Thick and Thin: Moral Argument at Home and Abroad* (Notre Dame, IN: University of Notre Dame Press, 2019)

Warren, C. *Supreme Court in United States History, 1856–1918, Volume III* (Washington, DC: Beard Books, 1999)

The We Company. 'Form S-1' (2019), https://www.sec.gov/Archives/edgar/data/1533523/000119312519220499/d781982ds1.htm accessed 6 Apr. 2020

Weil, S., Wills, A. (trans.). *The Need for Roots: Prelude to a Declaration of Duties towards Mankind* (London: Routledge, 2002)

West, E. *Small Men on the Wrong Side of History: The Decline, Fall, and Unlikely Return of Conservatism* (London: Constable, 2020)

Westcott, N. *Imperialism and Development: The East African Groundnut Scheme and Its Legacy* (James Currey, 2020)

Wilson, D. S. *This View of Life: Completing the Darwinian Revolution* (New York: Vintage Books, 2020)

Woolf, V. 'Mr. Bennett and Mrs. Brown' (London: The Hogarth Press, 1924)

Yehuda, R. et al. 'Transgenerational Effects of Post-traumatic Stress Disorder in Babies of Mothers Exposed to the World Trade Center

Attacks during Pregnancy', *Journal of Clinical Endocrinology & Metabolism*, Vol. 90, No. 7 (2005) 4115-18

Young, M. *The Rise of the Meritocracy 1870–2033: An Essay on Education and Society* (London: Thames and Hudson, 1958)

Young, M. 'Down with Meritocracy', *Guardian* (29 June 2001)

Zimmerman, E. *Smacked: A Story of White-Collar Ambition, Addiction, and Tragedy* (New York: Random House, 2020)

Index

abortion
  and conflicting rights (US) 35–6
  Northern Ireland 115
act utilitarianism 23–4
activism 40–42, 119
  and business purposes 132
  constructive 44–6
  environmentalism 41
  Extinction Rebellion xvii, 41
  Occupy movement 40–41
  and party leaders 120–21
  performative xviii, 41
  protest movements 44
  see also pressure groups, single
    issue
Adams, John, US President 79n
Adenauer, Konrad 66
age, and political allegiance 79–81
air travel, low cost 70
Airbnb 136
Airbus 126, 133
Allen, Bill, Boeing 110
Alliance Defending Freedom 40
altruism 26
Amazon 136
American Civil Liberties Union 40
American Enterprise Institute 15
Angelou, Maya 138
animals, domestic cats 96–7
Anscombe, Elizabeth 95
'anywheres', and meritocracy 84–7
Ardern, Jacinda, New Zealand
    prime minister xv
Aristotle 91, 101, 134

Arrow, K. J. and F. H. Hahn 14, 27
  General Competitive Analysis 13
artificial intelligence (AI), opportu-
    nities and dangers 123–4
associations 94–5, 152
  collective intelligence 113–14
  German *Verein* 143, 152
Athens 47, 155
Attlee, Clement 7, 118
Australia, and COVID-19 xv

banks
  loans 136–7
  regional 142–3
  see also finance sector
Barclays bank 117
Bausch Health 20
Becker, Gary 15–16, 113
Beeching, Richard 54
Benefits Street television series 52
Bentham, Jeremy 15, 16
  individualism 5
  and natural rights 35
  utilitarianism 23
Berlin Wall, opening of (1979) 71
Berlusconi, Silvio, overconfidence 110
Bevin, Ernest 84–5
Bezos, Jeff 31
Biden, Joe, US President xviii,
    xix, 65
Birmingham, University of 59
BlackRock 132
Blair, Margaret, and Lynn Stout
    128–9

Blair, Tony, prime minister 22, 72, 81–2
  influences on 102
Boesky, Ivan 4–5
bonuses 17, 70
Boot, Jesse 59
boundedness 103–4
Branson, Richard 17
Brexit referendum (2016) 65, 118
  response to 85
bribery 16
Bristol University 59
British Leyland 56
British Transport Commission 52, 54
Brown, Gordon 110
  as Chancellor of the Exchequer 82, 102
  prime minister 81
building societies, effect of privatisation 114
Burke, Edmund 94, 103
  on representative democracy 119, 120
Burlakoff, Alec, Insys 21
Bush, George H. W., US President 73
business
  branding and advertising 135
  and collective knowledge 125–6
  complexity of 61–2
  and local vocational training 149
  measures of success 131
  mediating hierarchy in 128–30
  and modern personal relations 136
  and motivation 125
  and profit 18, 30, 130–31
  purpose of 130–32
  and shareholder value 16–18
  and social responsibility 8, 22, 132, 152
  top-down management xxiii

business founders, and future wealth 31
Business Roundtable, US 131
Butskellism 66

California 43
  Public Employees Retirement Scheme 131
Callaghan, James, prime minister 72
Cameron, David, prime minister 84
  and 'Big Society' 103
'capacity to be productive', in regions 140, 149, 154
Carey, John, The Intelletuals and the Masses 82
Castro, Fidel 109
cats, domestic (Cattus Economicus) 96–7
celebrities
  expressive individualism 3
  and global causes 43
Central Electricity authority 52
centralization
  failures of 57–8
  nationalization as 52–6
  political 122
  and supply failures 62
  see also decentralization; hyper-centralization
CEOs
  remuneration 17, 18
  and social responsibility 132, 152
Chamberlain, Joseph, and University of Birmingham 59
charities 44–6
children
  early-years care and provision 146–8
  and gender dysphoria 39–40
  pre-schooling 148
  and schools 148–9
China, and COVID-19 xv
Christakis, Nicholas xxi, 96, 108
Chua, Amy 86

Churchill, Winston 101–2
cities and towns, broken 142
    and narratives of grievance 145
    recreating 149–50
citizen assemblies 119
Citizens United, US Supreme Court
        judgment 34–5
citizenship, and obligation 103–4
civic society 143
civil rights 37–48
    movement in America 37–8, 69
civil society 92
Clarke, Kenneth, MP 74
class
    and political allegiance 79–81
    somewheres and anywheres 84–7
    see also meritocracy; middle
        class; working class
climate change 25
    business and 132
Clinton, Bill, US President 30, 72
Clinton, Hillary, and 2016 election
        support 80
coal industry 53, 55
collective intelligence (knowledge)
        98–9, 119, 125–6, 155
    leadership and 110–111
Collier, Paul
    and Grissou (cat) 96–7
    The Future of Capitalism xiii
Collins, Jim, Built to Last (1994)
        19
common purpose 99–100, 107–11
    and shared identity 110–11
communication
    for common purpose 99–100,
        107–11
    human 6–7
communism
    fall of 14, 29, 71
    Western fear of 71
    working-class support for 71–2
communitarian governance 101–11
communitarian politics 112–24

communitarianism xxi–xxii, 155–6
    evolution of 94–5
    in human nature 91–100
communitarians
    philosophers 8, 94–5, 101
    in politics 101–3
community; communities 93–4
    and collective knowledge 98–9
    and empowerment 104
    and individualism 6
    and individuals 37
    and levels of trust 106–7
    and market 134–7
    mediation and cooperation 113–14
    as natural to humans 150
    and networks 99–100
    of place 138–50
    and rites of passage 47
    and rule-making 104
    small 103
    and social care 153
    and 'somewheres' 84–7
    see also local government
compassion 92
competition 61
    bounded 105–6
    and cooperation 99–100, 108–9
    and pluralism 105
Competition and Markets
        Authority 61n
computers, personal 70
Comte, Auguste 15, 16
conscription, non-military 86 and n
Conservative Party
    election of leader 120–21
    return of pragmatism 83–4
    see also Right, political
constructive activism 44–6
consumer goods 70
consumption, and self-expression
        46–7
cooperation
    and competition 99–100, 108–9
    and successful societies 4

cooperative movement 114
copyright 32, 33
Corbyn, Jeremy xix, 41, 72
  and 2019 election 76
  election as party leader 120
  expressive individualism 83
corruption 16
Cottam, Hilary 147, 148, 153
Coupe, Mike, Sainsbury's 61
COVID-19 pandemic
  centralized testing 57-8
  responses to xiii-xvi
  and social cohesion 154-5
credit
  consumer 68
  and trust 136-7
Crosland, Tony 53
  The Future of Socialism 51
Cruddas, Jon, MP, xix
Cuba, Kennedy and 109-10
'culture wars' xvi-xix

decentralization 98
  and financial autonomy 139,
    153-4
  and markets 61-3
  and participatory democracy 123
  and place 138
Declaration of Independence
    (American) 5
demand management 14
  and full employment 13
democracy
  direct 118
  inclusive 121-2
  industrial 133-4
  participatory 122-4, 151, 156
  representative 118-20
Democratic Party (US) 7-8
Denmark, and COVID-19 xv, xxii
depression
  and loneliness 152, 156
  and possessive individualism
    47

deregulation, finance sector 69-70
Dickens, Charles, Mrs Jellyby in
    Bleak House 42-3, 150
Disney Corporation 33
Disraeli, Benjamin 79
Don Valley
  and 2019 election 7, 65, 75
  and education 85
  loss of Labour support 76-7, 77
  members of parliament 121
Doyle, Andy 128
Drosten, Christian 58
drugs, marketing of 20-21
Dworkin, Ronald 35

East India Company 128
Easterbrook, F. H. and D. R. Fischel
    27
eBay 136
'Economic Man'
  and evolution 95-7
  as greedy and selfish 26-7, 92
  and market fundamentalism 14
economics
  governments and 22-3
  individualist 13-28
  market fundamentalism model
    26-8, 82
  modularity 126-8
  and politics 15
  tax and benefit system 82, 102, 140
  see also centralization; market
    fundamentalism; property
    rights
Edelman Survey, on trust in
    governments 63
Edinburgh
  civic society 143, 144n
  productive capacity 141
Edinburgh South constituency 79
education
  Academy and Charter schools 72
  German tertiary 143
  and meritocracy 84-6

and move away from community
85–6
nationalization of higher 59–60
and political allegiance 79–81
right to 33–4
schools 148–9
vocational 146, 149
see also universities; vocational
training
Eisenhower, Dwight, US President
109
elderly, care for 152–3
elections
2019 general (UK) 7, 65, 75
see also Don Valley; Stoke-on-
Trent
electricity production, waste under
nationalization 54–5
Embery, Paul xviii–xix
employment
and demand management 13
productive local 146–9, 154
and workers' rights 133–4
empowerment, of community 104
En Marche movement, France 64
Enron 134
entitlement
intellectual 3
material 2
see also rights
Equality Act (2010) 39
Etzioni, Amitai 95, 102
eudaimonia ('deserving of love') 92
European Commission, regional
'structural funds' 122
expressive individualism xvi, 3, 5, 47–8
and good governance 101
of political left xvii, 83
of rich 79
see also activism; self-expression
Extinction Rebellion xvii, 41

Fabian Society 15*n*
Facebook 136

fairness 101
human concept of 97
feeling, intensity of
and activism 41, 42–3
and moral worth 3
Ferguson, Adam 93, 107–8
finance sector
deregulation 69–70
need for social responsibility 152
and regional autonomy 142–3
rise of 69–70
financial autonomy, and decentralization 139, 153–4
financial crisis (2008) 27, 41, 69
legal prosecutions 117
and loans 137
Fink, Larry, BlackRock 132
Finland, education 149
Firth, Mark, and University of
Sheffield 59
Fiscal Responsibility Act (2010) 116
Flint, Caroline, MP 84*n*, 85
Florida, Richard 80
Ford, Henry 110
Forrester, John, MP 121–2
foster care 147
France xx
2017 presidential election 64
and COVID-19 xvi
Fourth Republic 67
post-war prosperity 67
pre-school *écoles maternelles* 148
Franco, General 66
free-riders, and concept of fairness
97, 103
Friedman, Milton 18, 26, 30, 134
further education *see* vocational
training
Future Wellbeing Act (2010),
Wales 116

Ganesh, Janan 140*n*
gap years 86
gas industry, national grid 53

Gates, Bill, Microsoft 17
Gates, Bill and Melinda 44
Gaulle, General de 67
gay rights 40
gender dysphoria 39–40, 43
General Electric Company 56
General Social Care Council 147
Germany 71, 122
  2017 election 64
  COVID-19 testing 58
  and former East Germany 71,
    141, 144–5
  local business organizations 143
  local leadership 144
  nuclear industry 42
  post-war recovery 67
  regional autonomy 141, 142
Gilets Jaune protests 64
Glasgow, electoral support 78
Glendon, Mary Ann 35, 36
global salvationism 22–3, 24–6
globalization 74
  and modern personal relations
    136
Goodhart, David 25
  The Road to Somewhere 85
Google 136
Gordon, Robert 70
Gorsky, Alex, Johnson & Johnson
  131
Gove, Michael 105
governance, communitarian
  101–11
governments
  declining trust in 25–6
  and global salvationism 22–3,
    24–6
  and industry 56–7
  lack of commercial ability 61–2,
    74
  lack of trust in 63
  need for decentralization 153–4
  and public provision 24, 155–6
  see also state

'greed is good' 4–5
  and economic potential 27
  and shareholder interests 131
Green Party, Germany 42
Greenspan, Alan, chairman of
  Federal Reserve 28
Groundnuts Scheme 53–4
'groupthink' 109

Hain, Peter, on loss of Labour
  support 77–8
Hale, Lady, Supreme Court 115
Handy, Charles 125
Hankins, James xxii
Hardin, Garrett 32
Hatton, Derek 72
Healey, Denis 81
Heath, Edward 55
Hegel, Georg 94
Henderson, Rebecca xx
Henrich, Joe xxi, 98, 108
Heritage Foundation 15
Heseltine, Michael, MP 78*n*
hierarchy
  authoritarian 130
  mediating 128–30
Hofer, Norbert, Austrian Freedom
  Party 8
'holarchy', 'holacracy', holons
  127–8
Holmes, Oliver Wendell 35
households, mediation of interests
  113
housing
  and 'right to buy' 83
  working class aspirations 82–3
human nature
  communitarianism in 91–100
  and mutuality 3
  pursuit of happiness 92
human rights 33–5
  legal assertion of 114
  and property rights 34–5
Hume, David xvii–xviii, 94

Hungarian Revolution (1956)
71
'The Hydro' electricity supplier
114
hyper-centralization 139–41

Iacocca, Lee 17
identity, personal 138–9
identity politics 1
  and business 133
imagination
  creative 98
  and language 6–7
India, and COVID-19 xv
individualism
  Bentham and 5
  and clash of interests 113
  and community 6
  and erosion of communitarian
    governance 101–2
  extreme 1
  ideologies of 7
  and loneliness 156
  and self-expression 46–7
  see also expressive individualism;
    possessive individualism;
    utilitarian individualism
industrial democracy 133–4
industrial relations, coal industry
  55
Industrial Reorganization
  Corporation (IRC) 56
inequality, post-war reduction 68
inflation, 1970s 14, 69
innovations, technological 70
Institute of Economic Affairs 15
Insys pharmaceuticals 20–21
intellectual entitlement 3
intellectual property rights 32
internet 70
  and modern personal relations
    136
investors 129
  see also shareholders

Italy
  political instability 67
  populist government 64–5

Jackson, Andrew 112
Jacobs, Jane 138, 151
Janis, Irving 109
Jenkins, Roy, and social reforms 44
Jensen, M. C., and W. H. Meckling
  27
Johnson & Johnson 19, 20, 21, 131
Johnson, Boris, prime minister 8,
  84, 121
  pragmatic approach to working
    class 86–7
Johnson, Lyndon, US President 37,
  69
Johnson, R. W. 19, 110
judicial review, increased scope of
  115
justice
  and market fundamentalism 30
  and rights 29–30
  see also law

Kaczyński, Jaroslaw, Polish party
  leader 8
Kay, John, and Mervyn King,
  Radical Uncertainty xiii
Keele University 59, 85
Kellaway, Lucy 45–6
Kendall, Liz, MP 152–3
Kennedy, Justice Anthony 37
Kennedy, John F., US President 1
  and leadership 109–10
Kennedy, Robert 110
Kensington, Labour 2019 election
  victory 79
Keynes, John Maynard 91
  The General Theory of Employ-
    ment, Interest and Money
    (1936) 13
King, Martin Luther 37
Kinnock, Neil 81

'knowing the model' 26–8, 82, 97–9
knowledge, collective 98–9, 119,
    125–6, 155
Koestler, Arthur 127 and *n*
Kopp, Wendy, Teach for America 45

Labour governments
    1945–51: nationalization 52–3,
        66, 75
    1960s–1970s 56, 72
    New Labour (1997–2010) 57,
        72, 83
Labour Party 7
    and 2019 election 7, 65
    commitment to nationalization
        53, 60
    and communist extremists 72
    election of leader 120
    Hartlepool by-election xix
    and individualism 81
    and loss of working-class
        support xviii–xix, xxii, 75–87
    as party of underclass 81
    and rise of meritocracy 81–2
    see also Left, political
Land Registry 114 and *n*
language, and imagination 6–7
law
    adversarial court system 116–17
    and politics 115–17
    see also justice
lawyers, and privatization 114
Le Pen, Marine xx
leadership 107–11
    communication 108
    cooperation and competition
        108–9
    local 144, 145
    modesty 110
    overconfidence 110
    use of coercion 108
    wartime 107
Left, political xviii–xix
    abandonment of socialism 71–2

in Europe 66
and fall of communism 14
and individual rights 29
moral superiority 83–4
origin of term 66
and working class 7–8
see also Labour Party; socialism
legislation, declaratory 115–16
Liberal Democrats, referendum
    118
liberty, and individual rights 37
Limbaugh, Rush 2
Lindsay, A. D. 59
Liverpool
    Liverpool Walton constituency
        76, 78–9
    Toxteth riots 78*n*
local government 60
    decline of 122
    elected mayors 144
    Treasury control over 139
    see also regions
Locke, John, on property rights 2
London
    hyper-centralization 139–41
    Little Village charity 46, 138
    and need for decentralization
        154
    and well-being score 140 and *n*
London Transport 53
loneliness 152, 156
lottery winners 47

McGowan, Harry, ICI 17
MacGregor, Neil 47
MacIntyre, Alasdair 35, 95, 102
Macmillan, Harold 67
Macmurray, John 101, 102
    Persons in Relations 101
Macpherson, C. B. 95, 102, 134
Macron, Emmanuel, French
    president xx, 8, 64, 110
Major, John, prime minister 73
Manchester, University of 59

Mandelson, Peter, MP 81–2
Mao Zedong, and Great Leap
    Forward 104–5
market economies, disciplined
    pluralism in 62–3
market fundamentalism 4, 8
    and 'Economic Man' 14
    and economic shocks 28
    and knowing the model 26–8,
    97–9
    and property rights 5
    and shareholder interests 131
marketplaces, as centre of
    communities 134–5
markets 16
    Adam Smith and 7
    and community 8–9, 134–7
    and decentralization 61–3
    and public provision 24
    relationships 94
    in untradeable property 16, 35
Marx, Karl 15, 16, 95
Maslow, Abraham 92–3
material entitlement 2
Matthews, Robin 13–14
Mattision, Deborah xix
May, Theresa, prime minister 84
Mayer, Colin xxi
media, London influence 154
Merck, George 19, 110, 131, 150
Merck Pharmaceuticals 19–20,
    21
meritocracy 72
    and 'anywheres' 84–7
    and education 84–6
    pretensions of 82–4
    rise of 81–2
Merkel, Angela, German
    Chancellor 42
Mermaids charity 39–40, 43
#MeToo movement 35
metropolitan elite 86–7
middle class, and 1960s student
    protests 69, 79

Miliband, David 102
Miliband, Ed 102–3
Militant Tendency 72, 78n
Mill, John Stuart 23
Minogue, Kenneth 37–8
minorities, protection of 106
'Minus-One Club' 45
Mitterand, François, French
    president 71
mobile phones 70
models
    overconfident belief in xiii, xiv
    see also 'knowing the model'
modularity
    in business 126–8
    and development of collective
        intelligence 98–9
Momentum, extremist grouping 72
monitoring 22–3, 148
moral superiority, claims of 3, 83–4
More in Common, research group
    xvi
Morgan, J.P. 136
Morrison, Herbert 84–5
    and nationalization 53
Moynihan, Senator, US 143
mutuality
    humans and 3
    in participatory democracy 123–4

National Bread Service, hypo-
    thetical 61, 62, 105, 135
National Coal Board 52
National Council for Civil Liberties
    39
National Enterprise Board 56
National Health Service (NHS) 52,
    57–8
    over-centralization 57–8
    planned IT system 57
    and social care 153
nationalization 52–6
Netherlands, home-helpers for
    mothers 147

networks 99–100
Neumann, Adam, WeWork 9, 152
New Zealand
  central bank 23
  and COVID-19 xv
'nexus of contracts' theory 129
Nixon, Richard, US President 1
Noble, Denis xxi
North Korea, and COVID-19 xxii
Northern Ireland, abortion law 115
Norway, sovereign wealth fund 131
Nottingham, University of 59
Nozick, Robert 32, 91
  Anarchy, State and Utopia 30–31

Obama, Barack, US President 2, 4, 72
obligation, and citizenship 103–4
Ocasio-Cortez, Alexandria 65
Occupy movement 40–41
oil crisis (1973) 14, 69
Orbán, Viktor, Hungarian prime minister xv, 8
Osborne, George, Chancellor of the Exchequer 22, 102
  and local government 60
Ostrom, Elinor 32
  and boundedness 103–4
Owens, John, and Manchester University 59

Paedophile Information Exchange (PIE) 38–9
Parliament, as deliberative assembly 119–20
participatory democracy 122–4, 151, 156
partnerships, and privatization 114
Patel, Priti xvii, xviii
Pearson, Michael, Valeant Pharmaceuticals 20, 150
pension schemes, defined benefit 114
Pericles, funeral oration vii, 155

Perot, Ross 45
Peters, Tom, *Fast Company* 37
pharmaceutical industry 19–22, 152
philanthropy
  as constructive activism 44–6
  telescopic 42–3
place, communities of 138–50
play, and imagination 98
pluralism
  lacking in nationalized industries 54, 55, 58, 63
  in market economies 62–3
  protection and bounding of 104–6
political parties
  Britain 65*n*
  choice of leaders 120–21
  and decline of centre 68–70, 151
  lack of trust in 64–5
  and loss of contact with electorates 74, 151–2
  and single-issue pressure groups 65, 112–13
  see also Conservative Party; Labour Party; Left, political; Right, political
politicians
  careers 121, 151
  cultural and social distance from electorate 121–2
politics 151–2
  and centralization 122
  communitarian 112–24
  and the courts 115–17
  and decentralization 123
  and declaratory legislation 115–16
  inclusive 121–2
  and 'legally binding' policies 116
  and rise of individualism 112–13
possessive individualism 2, 4, 26–7
  and depression 47
  of Economic Man 14

and market fundamentalism 30–31
and property rights 31–2
power stations 54–5
Prague Spring (1968) 71
pressure groups, single issue 65, 112–13
and self-righteousness 112
see also activism
private sector, and common purpose 125
privatization 54, 55–6
and new property rights 114
pro-sociality 107
profit 18, 30, 130–31
pharmaceutical companies 19–22
property rights 5
and human rights 34–5
legitimate 33
Locke 2
origins of 31–3
and privatization 114
shareholders 30
prosperity, mass 67–8
public corporations, financial autonomy 54
Public Health England 57
public sector, and common purpose 125
public-sector workers
monitoring and incentives 22–3
and targets 23
Pulzer, Peter 78
Purdue Pharmaceuticals 20
Putnam, Robert xxi–xxii, 93, 106, 148–9

railways 52
failure of nationalization 54
Rajan, Raghu xxi
Ramsey, Frank 24
Rand Corporation 15n
rational choice, in economic models 26

Rawls, John xxi, 91, 93
A Theory of Justice 29–30
Reagan, Ronald, US President 73
referendums 118
regions
and decentralization 141
factors in prosperity 141–5
and need to rebalance 154
Right, political xx
libertarian 30–31
and market fundamentalism 8, 14, 73
origin of term 66
and pragmatic moderation 66–7, 73–4
problems of 73–4
see also Conservative Party
right to bear arms 36
rights 29–36
American and French revolutions 5, 35
assertion of 5
civil and political 33, 37, 38
conflicting claims to 35–6, 38–40, 113
'natural' 35
and obligations 34
social and economic 33
universalism of 91
see also civil rights; human rights; property rights
rights talk 35–6, 40
rites of passage 47
rituals, performative 123
Robbins Report (1963) 59–60
Rockefeller, John D. 61
Roe v. Wade 36
Rolls-Royce 56
Roosevelt, Eleanor 33
Roosevelt, Franklin, US President 00, 101
Rorty, Richard 95
Rousseau, Jean-Jacques 17
rule of law 101, 107

rule utilitarianism 23–4
rule-making, communities 104

Sacks, Jonathan xxi
Sainsbury's, and Asda 61
Salazar, António, Portugal 66
Salt, Sir Titus 44, 150
Saltaire 44
Salvini, Matteo, Italian Lega Nord
    leader 8
Samuelson, Paul 26
Sandel, Michael 35, 37, 95
    influence of 102–3
    The Tyranny of Merit xxi
    What Money Can't Buy 134
Sanders, Bernie 41, 65
Sargent, Thomas 27
Savage, L. J. 26
Scandinavia 86, 106–7
Scargill, Arthur 55, 72
Schettino, Francesco, *Costa
    Concordia* 108–9
Scotland 118
    public spending 144
    regional identity 142
    see also Edinburgh
Second World War, and national
    solidarity 51–2
self, emphasis on 6
self-expression
    and individualism 46–7
    performative 5
self-invention 47
selfishness, individual 91–2
    economic 15
    see also individualism
Seligman, Martin 93
Shackleton, Ernest 108–9
Shaftesbury, Earl of 44
shareholder value 16–18, 83
    drug companies 19
shareholders 129
    property rights of 30

Shaw, George Bernard 15n
Sheffield, University of 59
Shkreli, Martin, Turing
    Pharmaceuticals 20
Sidgwick, Henry 24
Silicon Valley 128
Simon, Herbert 126–7, 128
Singapore, and COVID-19 xv
Singer, Peter 24
Sloan, Alfred, General Motors 17,
    110
Sloan, David 103
Smeeth, Ruth, MP 84n, 85
Smith, Adam xvii, xix, 7, 92
    on community and market 135
    The Wealth of Nations 94
    Theory of Moral Sentiments 93,
    94
Smuts, Jan 127 and n
SNP, and referendum on secession
    118
social capital 106–7
social care 152–3
social cohesion, and response to
    COVID-19 xiii–xvi, 154–5
social liberalism, and rights claims
    38
social reforms 44–5
social responsibility, and business
    8, 22, 132, 152
social welfare 24
social workers, scrutiny role of
    147–8
socialism
    in America 64, 65, 66
    in Britain 71, 72
    in Europe 68, 71–2
    and mass prosperity 67–8
    see also Left, political
society
    cooperation and competition 4
    interrelationships 3–4
Sombart, Werner 64, 67

'somewheres', and community 84–7
South Korea, and COVID-19 xv
Soviet Union
  central planning 51, 61
  disintegration 14, 29
  perception of techological power
    66, 71
Sparta 155
stakeholders
  in business 131–2
  and industrial democracy 133
standard of living, right to 33
Starmer, Keir xix
states
  and central planning 51
  effect of Second World War on 51
  limits on 155–6
  and upholding of rights 29, 34
  see also governments
Stoke-on-Trent
  and 2019 election 7, 65, 75
  and Keele University 59, 85
  loss of Labour support 76–7,
    77
  members of parliament 121–2
subsidiarity 104, 156
suicide 47 and n
Sumption, Jonathan, Lord 115
supply failures, in centralized
    economies 62
Swayne, Justice 16, 35
Sweden
  conscription 86 and n
  and COVID-19 xv
  rightist coalition 73
  social democracy 71
Switzerland 86
  participatory democracy 123
  vocational training 149

Taiwan, and COVID-19 xv
tax and benefit system 82, 102
  and regional inequality 140

Taylor, Charles 95
Teach for America 45
Teach First 45
technology
  economic consequences 74
  post-war innovation 70
telephone network, privatization
    55–6
telescopic philanthropy 42–3
territorial rights 31
Thatcher, Margaret, prime minister
  73
  and new universities 60
  and trade unions 55
Thornberry, Emily, MP 84n
Thucydides 155
Tocqueville, Alexis de, Democracy
  in America 94–5
Todd, Ron, union leader 67–8
trade unions, effect of privatization
    114
'tragedy of the commons' 32, 103–4
transgender rights 39–40
TripAdvisor 136
Truman, Harry S., US President 7
Trump, Donald, US President
  8, 75
  and 2016 election support 80
  appeal to working class 86
  election of 64
  and individualism 2–3
  overconfidence 110
trust
  levels of 106–7
  and personal contact 138
Turing Pharmaceuticals 20
Turner, Lane 2

Uber 136
uncertainty 7
  and economic shocks 26, 27
  radical xiii, xiv, xx, xxi,
    xxii–xxiii, 39, 104, 108, 117

United Kingdom
  centralization 52–6, 57–8, 122
  City-Region Combined Authorities 142
  hyper-centralization 139–41
  post-war prosperity 67–8
  post-war statism 51
  regional economic divergence 139–40
  and regional identity 142
  response to COVID-19 xiv
  see also London
United Nations, Declaration of Human Rights (1948) 5, 33–4
United States of America
  Capitol Hill rioters xvi, xviii
  civil rights movement 37–8
  conflicting rights 36
  election of Trump 64
  political interpretation of Constitution 117
  political left 68–9
  political parties 65
  political supporters 80–81
  presidential speeches 1–2
  response to COVID-19 xvi
  suicide 47n
  working class voters 7–8
  see also US Supreme Court
universities 146
  conversion of polytechnics to 60
  and local civic society 143
  local origins of 59
  new campuses 60
University Grants Committee 59
US Supreme Court
  Citizens United judgment (2010) 34–5
  judgments on gay rights 40
  Planned Parenthood v. *Casey* 37
  political appointments 117
utilitarian individualism 5, 23–6

Valeant Pharmaceuticals 20
Vanuatu, rite of passage 47
Verein, German clubs and associations 143, 152
Vietnam War, America and 69
vocational training 146, 149

Wales, lack of finance industry 143
Wall Street (film) 5
Walmart 62
Walzer, Michael 37, 95
  Spheres of Justice 134
water boards, regional 114
wealth, sources of 31–2
Webb, Sidney and Beatrice 15n
Weil, Simone 29
Welch, Jack, GEC 17
welfare state 66
Wells, H. G. 15n
Welsh government, declaratory legislation 116
WeWork 8–9
Whitman, Walt 1
Wilberforce, William 44
Wills family, Bristol 59
women
  improved lives of 68
  rights of 39
Woolf, Virginia 82–3
workforce, motivation of 16–17
working class
  distance from meritocracy 82–3
  and metropolitan elite 86–7
  and politics 7–8
World Trade Center, 9/11 attacks, and maternal stress 146–7
World Values Survey 106

Young, Michael 75, 81, 84

Zappos shoe retailer 127, 128

ALLEN LANE
an imprint of
PENGUIN BOOKS

Also Published

Robin DiAngelo, *Nice Racism: How Progressive White People Perpetuate Racial Harm*

Rosemary Hill, *Time's Witness: History in the Age of Romanticism*

Lawrence Wright, *The Plague Year: America in the Time of Covid*

Adrian Wooldridge, *The Aristocracy of Talent: How Meritocracy Made the Modern World*

Julian Hoppit, *The Dreadful Monster and its Poor Relations: Taxing, Spending and the United Kingdom, 1707-2021*

Jordan Ellenberg, *Shape: The Hidden Geometry of Absolutely Everything*

Duncan Campbell-Smith, *Crossing Continents: A History of Standard Chartered Bank*

Jemma Wadham, *Ice Rivers*

Niall Ferguson, *Doom: The Politics of Catastrophe*

Michael Lewis, *The Premonition: A Pandemic Story*

Chiara Marletto, *The Science of Can and Can't: A Physicist's Journey Through the Land of Counterfactuals*

Suzanne Simard, *Finding the Mother Tree: Uncovering the Wisdom and Intelligence of the Forest*

Giles Fraser, *Chosen: Lost and Found between Christianity and Judaism*

Malcolm Gladwell, *The Bomber Mafia: A Story Set in War*

Kate Darling, *The New Breed: How to Think About Robots*

Serhii Plokhy, *Nuclear Folly: A New History of the Cuban Missile Crisis*

Sean McMeekin, *Stalin's War*

Michio Kaku, *The God Equation: The Quest for a Theory of Everything*

Michael Barber, *Accomplishment: How to Achieve Ambitious and Challenging Things*

Charles Townshend, *The Partition: Ireland Divided, 1885-1925*

Hanif Abdurraqib, *A Little Devil in America: In Priase of Black Performance*

Carlo Rovelli, *Helgoland*

Herman Pontzer, *Burn: The Misunderstood Science of Metabolism*

Jordan B. Peterson, *Beyond Order: 12 More Rules for Life*

Bill Gates, *How to Avoid a Climate Disaster: The Solutions We Have and the Breakthroughs We Need*

Kehinde Andrews, *The New Age of Empire: How Racism and Colonialism Still Rule the World*

Veronica O'Keane, *The Rag and Bone Shop: How We Make Memories and Memories Make Us*

Robert Tombs, *This Sovereign Isle: Britain In and Out of Europe*

Mariana Mazzucato, *Mission Economy: A Moonshot Guide to Changing Capitalism*

Frank Wilczek, *Fundamentals: Ten Keys to Reality*

Milo Beckman, *Math Without Numbers*

John Sellars, *The Fourfold Remedy: Epicurus and the Art of Happiness*

T. G. Otte, *Statesman of Europe: A Life of Sir Edward Grey*

Alex Kerr, *Finding the Heart Sutra: Guided by a Magician, an Art Collector and Buddhist Sages from Tibet to Japan*

Edwin Gale, *The Species That Changed Itself: How Prosperity Reshaped Humanity*

Simon Baron-Cohen, *The Pattern Seekers: A New Theory of Human Invention*

Christopher Harding, *The Japanese: A History of Twenty Lives*

Carlo Rovelli, *There Are Places in the World Where Rules Are Less Important Than Kindness*

Ritchie Robertson, *The Enlightenment: The Pursuit of Happiness 1680-1790*

Ivan Krastev, *Is It Tomorrow Yet?: Paradoxes of the Pandemic*

Tim Harper, *Underground Asia: Global Revolutionaries and the Assault on Empire*

John Gray, *Feline Philosophy: Cats and the Meaning of Life*

Priya Satia, *Time's Monster: History, Conscience and Britain's Empire*

Fareed Zakaria, *Ten Lessons for a Post-Pandemic World*

David Sumpter, *The Ten Equations that Rule the World: And How You Can Use Them Too*

Richard J. Evans, *The Hitler Conspiracies: The Third Reich and the Paranoid Imagination*

Fernando Cervantes, *Conquistadores*

John Darwin, *Unlocking the World: Port Cities and Globalization in the Age of Steam, 1830-1930*

Michael Strevens, *The Knowledge Machine: How an Unreasonable Idea Created Modern Science*

Owen Jones, *This Land: The Story of a Movement*

Seb Falk, *The Light Ages: A Medieval Journey of Discovery*

Daniel Yergin, *The New Map: Energy, Climate, and the Clash of Nations*

Michael J. Sandel, *The Tyranny of Merit: What's Become of the Common Good?*

Joseph Henrich, *The Weirdest People in the World: How the West Became Psychologically Peculiar and Particularly Prosperous*

Leonard Mlodinow, *Stephen Hawking: A Memoir of Friendship and Physics*

David Goodhart, *Head Hand Heart: The Struggle for Dignity and Status in the 21st Century*

Claudia Rankine, *Just Us: An American Conversation*

James Rebanks, *English Pastoral: An Inheritance*

Robin Lane Fox, *The Invention of Medicine: From Homer to Hippocrates*

Daniel Lieberman, *Exercised: The Science of Physical Activity, Rest and Health*

Sudhir Hazareesingh, *Black Spartacus: The Epic Life of Touissaint Louverture*